Chicago DisASterS

Bryan W. Alaspa

Schiffer Publishing Ltd

4880 Lower Valley Road · Atglen, PA · 19310

Schiffer Books are available at special discounts for bulk purchases for sales promotions or premiums. Special editions, including personalized covers, corporate imprints, and excerpts can be created in large quantities for special needs. For more information contact the publisher:

Published by Schiffer Publishing Ltd.
4880 Lower Valley Road
Atglen, PA 19310
Phone: (610) 593-1777; Fax: (610) 593-2002
E-mail: Info@schifferbooks.com

For the largest selection of fine reference books on this and related subjects, please visit our web site at **www.schifferbooks.com**
We are always looking for people to write books on new and related subjects. If you have an idea for a book please contact us at the above address.

This book may be purchased from the publisher.
Include $5.00 for shipping.
Please try your bookstore first.
You may write for a free catalog.

In Europe, Schiffer books are distributed by
Bushwood Books
6 Marksbury Ave.
Kew Gardens
Surrey TW9 4JF England
Phone: 44 (0) 20 8392-8585; Fax: 44 (0) 20 8392-9876
E-mail: info@bushwoodbooks.co.uk
Website: www.bushwoodbooks.co.uk

Cover photo: Blizzard © Mark Stout. Courtesy bigstockphoto.com
Text © Bryan W. Alaspa
Note: Wikipedia made up a small portion of research collected.

Designed by RoS
Type set in Decaying/Century Schoolbook

ISBN: 978-0-7643-3395-8

Printed in The United States of America

Dedication

For my grandmother, Jane.

Contents

Introduction
The Elemental City

The city known as Chicago is a city that was born in blood. It first began as a field of wild onions giving the city its name: "Chekagou." This name first began appearing on maps as early as 1684. By 1779, the area was known as a trading post owned by a man named Jean Baptist du Sable. The established trading post was sold and, before long, America began to expand westward. What was once in French hands was now in American hands. The trading post eventually became a fort known as Fort Dearborn.

The fort itself was not especially impressive for a while. The walls of the fort are probably what most people imagine when they think about forts. It was a pile of logs sharpened at the top and placed side to side. At the outermost wall, there was a solid wall and a gate at the entrance. To add to the mystique of the place, there was an underground entrance that ran all the way to the river. Once inside the fort, a soldier would have found a parade ground, quarters for officers, barracks for soldiers, a guard house, and a store house for ammunition.

The Birth of A City

By 1810, the fort was manned by a Captain Nathan Heald. He was a man well-respected with years of experience behind him. He was also no stranger to the frontier, which Chicago, or Fort Dearborn, still was at that point. Things ran well for a couple of years until the War of 1812 broke out.

The war had ravaged the Indian lands in America. The Indian tribes in and around Fort Dearborn were aggravated and easily roused. Many of them had decided to form alliances with British forces after determining that the rest of the Americans were invaders and not allies. The British captured a garrison at Mackinac and it looked like the next fort on the list was Fort Dearborn. Heald soon received orders from General William Hull that he should abandon the fort and leave everything behind. In fact, the orders specifically stated to leave everything to the Indian tribes.

Heald made a serious mistake and he delayed in giving the orders for the evacuation. The tribes moved in and the troops at the fort were surrounded. They had nowhere to go. As the terrified soldiers watched from around their walls the largest contingent of Indian tribes arrived and sieged the fort. The soldiers began expressing their concern to their superiors. Heald took one look at the numbers amassing outside his window and realized that negotiating might be the best bet.

So, on August 12th, Heald and a few of his officers marched out of the fort and had council with the Indians. It is estimated by those who witnessed this that there were some 500 Indians camped outside. Heald proposed to the Indian chief that he would distribute what stores were left at the fort along with ammunition in exchange for safe passage to Fort Wayne. The chiefs agreed.

Heald thought he had achieved something that would benefit everyone. He probably figured he would be greeted as a wise hero upon returning to the fort. Instead his remaining officers confronted him. They questioned his wisdom in offering the terms. They felt that all of the stores and ammunition could just be used against them and Heald caved in again. He and his officers broke apart the weapons and the extra ammunition and dumped them down a well. The stores of whiskey were emptied into a nearby river. This was easily noticed by the Indians outside the fort and they decided that, since Heald had not kept to his side of bargain, they didn't need to either, and they began making their own plans.

It looked like things were going to explode, but instead, on August 14th, the fort received a surprise. A Captain William Wells managed to get himself and thirty Miami warriors past the Indians outside and right to the front gate. Wells was also another frontier legend and he had decent relations with settlers and Indians in the area. He had, in fact, been captured by Indians as a child and raised by them. Wells spoke to the Indians outside and a second council was held.

Once again it looked like things were going to be okay. The Indians expressed their anger at the stores and ammunition being dumped but agreed to allow safe passage to Fort Wayne. Heald was told he and his men would need to abandon the fort immediately. Since his last effort, it was more than just Heald and his men he had to worry about. Families whose homes had been raided were also arriving at the fort. There was now a caravan of soldiers, horses, wagons, families, and animals ready to receive their safe passage to Fort Wayne.

The column of humanity was being escorted out of the fort and away by nearly 500 Potawatomi Indians. They marched in a southward direction in a column of clanking carts and anxious soldiers. Hardly anyone noticed as the Potawatomi escorts began moving quietly to the right, subtly putting an elevation of sand between them and the column of people and provisions.

The entire column of people and Indians reached the area that is now 16th Street and Indiana Avenue. Suddenly, the scouts and guides began milling around with each other at the front of the column. No sooner did this happen than all hell began to break out at the rear of the column. Captain Wells raised an alarm that the Indians were attacking. The soldiers were caught completely off-guard. The officers managed to rally and form the soldiers into battle formations. It was a valiant effort, but it was already too late. As the Indians began firing down on the column, so many men fell in the first rounds that giant holes were ripped in the line. The Indians were too numerous and they swarmed around the column of men, women, horses, and carts.

A Plan Gone Bad

What happened next was sheer slaughter. Not only were men cut down, they were brutally hacked to pieces. Officers were tomahawked. The fort's surgeon was shot down in a hail of bullets and literally cut into pieces. The wife of one soldier was seen fighting valiantly but was then hacked into bits before finally falling. Mrs. Heald was wounded by gunfire but spared by an Indian chief who was sympathetic to her. By the time the garrison surrendered, 148 members of the column lay dead in the field. Eighty-six of the dead were adults and twelve were children.

Captain Wells managed to survive the massacre and was taken prisoner. He was so enraged at the deaths and the carnage that he fought his way through his captors, found a horse, and took off. A hail of bullets greeted him but he managed to evade them. His horse was not so lucky and the animal fell. Two Indian chiefs stepped forward to plead for the life of Wells, but Pesotum, a Potawatomi chief, stabbed Wells in the back and killed him. His heart was then cut out and distributed to the various Indian warriors as a sign of bravery. His body was eventually buried in the sand near the lake.

Captain Heald also managed to survive. He was wounded twice while his wife was wounded seven times during the massacre. They were eventually turned over to a British commander at Mackinac who then sent them to Detroit. They were then exchanged with the Americans.

The rest of the survivors were taken prisoner. They were not treated well and many died as they were moved about. Some of them were sold to British soldiers as slaves, although they were soon released as the British were appalled by the tales of the massacre and not keen on accepting slaves. The bodies of those who died were left where they were for the animals and the elements to eventually erase.

The fort itself was set on fire. The Indians celebrated their victory as the logs and the remnants of the fort were burned. Replacement troops would eventually arrive at Fort Dearborn's location a year later. They found the ground burned and dozens of skeletons scattered about the remains. The soldiers buried what bones were left and rebuilt the fort which was eventually abandoned for the last time in 1836.

Boomtown

This was the birth of one of the greatest American cities. It was a story of blood and death that would seem to follow the development of Chicago at almost every step. Whether it was gangsters or murderers or serial killers, the blood has always flowed easily in the streets of Chicago. In those cases, including that of the Indian massacre, these were very much man-made disasters. This too is something that has haunted the history of Chicago.

Chicago eventually became a boomtown. Like so many with that label, this brought problems that would ultimately lead to the deaths of far too many Chicago's citizens. Chicago has had its share of natural disasters, man-made disasters, and anything and everything in between. Disasters from the air have followed those of growing much too quickly, disasters of water and, of course, fire.

While the area surrounding Chicago is relatively flat and free from fault lines, there have even been disasters of earth, where the sheer force of the planet itself brought about tragedy and change for the entire city.

Chicago remains one of the greatest cities of the world. It was one of the first to have skyscrapers. It introduced the hot dog to the world. It launched the world to Ferris wheels. But Chicago has earned its reputation as an elemental city born from the earth and experiencing disasters of water, air, fire, and earth.

One of the most famous, of course, was the fire that nearly stopped the city before it had the time to start growing.

Follow along as you are taken through the elements that Chicago represents.

Part One

City of Fire

Chicago has one of the best art museums the world has ever known. It has a world-renowned skyline. It has a park near the lake designed by a world-famous designer. It has a celebrated orchestra. It has one of the busiest airports on the planet. In short, Chicago has become a city that could rival any city anywhere in the world.

However, like most cities, it did not reach that level easily. It had to go through a number of growing pains. Just like cities such as New York, London, and others, there was a time when the city was growing faster than it was capable of sustaining safety. This was very true when the city first began the population explosion, and people were building houses out of wood to build them fast so that they would be able to keep up with the city's growing needs. Overcrowded and trying hard to catch up with the population explosion, Chicago was about to be baptized by fire.

Of course, like other cities, once the disaster hit, the changes were made that other cities followed. This is a story that would occur time and again as Chicago grew. As advancements were made, tragedy would strike, and the world would respond by making improvements. The cost for this was the lives of several hundred people, including entire families.

At the same time, misinformation has crept into the legends that surround Chicago. Many people know the story of the cow and the lantern, and have accepted it as truth. What they don't know is that things were much more complicated than that. Many may know about the safety precautions in theaters around the world, but they may not know the high cost in women and children that lead to those rules. And there are those who take for granted the fire protections in local schools, but most probably don't know how Chicago lead the way at the cost of so many of its children.

This is the story of how Chicago became a city of fire.

Chapter One

Cows, Lanterns, Legends, and Fire

The Great Chicago Fire is a legendary disaster and most people don't know the entire story. They think they know, of course. Almost everyone has heard the tale of Mrs. O'Leary's cow knocking over a lantern. But the full extent of the damage goes way beyond, perhaps even picturing some modern version of the city blazing against the night sky. What they don't realize is that, while indeed this was one of the greatest disasters in American history, without the fire, the city of Chicago might not have become the city it is today.

Enough Wood for a Fire

The fire started in 1871, during a time when Chicago was growing faster than anyone could have predicted. As far as the country went, Chicago was almost as far west as you could go. Yes, there were cities such as San Francisco along the western coast, but Chicago was really the biggest city before entering the frontier. It was a city where the buildings were crawling up into the sky and the land was slowly moving further and further into Lake Michigan. While the Colombian Exposition, or World's Fair, was still a few years away, Chicago was growing faster than the city planners could figure out how to manage.

There were those in the city who could see that the town was headed for trouble. The summer of the fire was a particularly hot and dry one. Several of the city's newspapers had called for stricter building codes and to increase the size of the fire department. There were plans in the works to make the city more fire-proof, but those plans were mired in bureaucratic red-tape.

Chicago had grown so fast that it was a ramshackle-looking city at this point. In fact, it was a city constructed primarily of wood. Rundown and leaning wooden buildings lined the roads as people tried to wedge themselves into neighborhoods already overcrowded.

Even the sidewalks and portions of the streets were wooden or covered with wooden planks. Chicago had become a major inland port and the docks were wood with wooden boats parked at the piers. The apartment buildings, houses, and office buildings had large portions made out of wood. There was even a large amount of wood piled up along docks along the Chicago River in barges because of a lumber mill right near the water. In short, this was a city looking for trouble.

As mentioned, that summer had been particularly hot and dry. Fires had begun relatively early as the city entered the dry and hot season known throughout the Midwest. City planners, city activists, and neighborhood leaders began to worry that things could get out of control. They asked the city for changes and they were told changes would come, perhaps in place as soon as the following summer.

Call boxes littered the city. These boxes would send a signal to a dispatcher who would then note the area of the city where the call was coming from and send out the appropriate fire station. To help, the city was also dotted with what amounted to lookouts. Fire departments manned these towers and it was the job of the lookouts to peer into the hot dark night and look for what could be fires in the distance. They too had what amounted to call boxes in their towers to then ring the right department, depending on the neighborhood. It was hardly a flawless system and it was prone to human error constantly.

The summer before had been a hot and dry one as well. The Chicago Fire Department had been kept very busy. At one time the previous summer, the city was experiencing two fires a day. The week leading up to the big fire had been taxing on the men designated to fight the blazes. There had been twenty fires preceding October 8, 1871.

In fact, the previous night, a major fire had been battled well into the wee hours by firefighters who would, eventually, be charged with trying to battle the big conflagration. The wind had played havoc with the fire that night. The wood was so dry in the buildings surrounding the area that the firefighters thought that the fire of that Saturday would burn out of control. The fire itself was not far from the O'Leary home and threatened to burn down much of the southern portion of the city. The firefighters battled bravely and, as Sunday dawned, they managed to calm the fire and then trudge wearily back toward their fire stations for some rest. Their equipment still bore the scorch marks from the previous night's fire and the smell of smoke clung to their clothes and hair. It burned through their noses as they collapsed in their beds and the lookouts took their watch for that Sunday evening.

Again, the evening was hot and dry with a high wind out of the south, which would send any flames toward the north. The lookouts scanned the city. Special attention was to be paid toward the area where the previous night's fire had been. Although the fire was out, the fire chiefs and those in the area were worried about embers and potential flare-ups during the heat of Sunday and the winds.

Confusion

The day went by without much incident. The weary firefighters took advantage of that to rest. Then, at about nine o'clock that night, a glow was spotted on the horizon. One of the lookouts contacted a dispatcher but the dispatcher was confused. He thought that the blaze was being reported in the same area as the fire from the previous night. Although not far from the O'Leary home, it was just far enough away that a different firefighting unit would need to be called. Thus, the wrong call was made to the wrong place.

The winds were blowing that night. The embers inside the barn were blown around the dry hay and even-drier wood. The fire did, indeed, start within the barn located on the property owned by Patrick and Catherine O'Leary. However, the fact seems to be that the O'Learys were sound asleep when the blaze started and it had nothing to do with Mrs. O'Leary trying to milk her cow by candlelight and an accident with the cow causing the blaze. By testimony given by the O'Leary's after the fire, they were as surprised as everyone else when their barn caught fire.

By the time the problems with calling the right fire department were sorted out, the barn was completely engulfed. There was no saving it. The wind was blowing the burning embers toward the center of the city. As those embers landed on other dried timber, hay, and grass, the blaze began to grow. Not far from where the O'Learys slept there was a party, and soon, members of that party were outside watching the fires. Given the commonplace feeling of fires at that time, there was no initial cause for concern. As the fire trucks eventually clanked and rattled their way down the streets, others were soon awakened and watching from windows and lining the streets to catch a glimpse of the firefighters and the blaze.

The call that finally summoned the right fire depart-ment didn't come through until 9:40 p.m. At first, the dis-patcher sent the right firefighters in the wrong direction. Once that was corrected, the fire was too big for the first team of firefighters to do much. By the time they reached the area where the fire was burning, the flames had spread to neighboring houses and sheds. The winds had picked up and the fire began moving north-eastward in a direction that would take it through the very heart of the city of Chicago. As the heat grew, the flames themselves created their own weather. (These days, that type of phenomenon is known as a "firestorm" where the flames themselves burn so intensely that they create whirlwinds that further drive the fires.)

The existing winds plus the winds created by the super-heated air created a fire that the firefighters, who were now arriving from all over the city, could not foresee and were powerless to control. The fire seemed like some tentacled monster slowly reaching out arms in directions that no fireman or fire chief could predict. As such, the firefighters couldn't get ahead of the blaze and attempt to contain it. As soon as they felt that they had cut off its path, the embers and winds would blow debris high into the air, creating new blazes behind and ahead of them. The fire proved capable of jumping streets and even rivers.

Panic Sets In

Soon, it became evident to those who were standing around expecting a show that things were getting out of con-trol. As one house and shed after another suddenly burst into flames, those who had thought they were in for an evening's entertainment began to panic. Those with homes in the path of the fire began trying to get home, but instead they clogged the streets. Others in the path began heading for the Chicago River, convinced that being near water, any water, would provide them with some kind of protection. Indeed, even those attempting to fight the blaze had hopes that the river would provide a kind of break for the flames. They couldn't have been more wrong.

The fire had started somewhere around nine at night. By ten and eleven o'clock, the streets were packed with people who were no longer watching with interest but fleeing for their lives. All around them houses exploded into flames. In the sky there were burning embers and debris landing all around them. The sidewalks themselves were bursting into flames wherever there was wood planking instead of dirt. The air was blazing hot and creating typhoon-like wind, burning lungs, hair, clothing, and anything else in its path. It was as if the air itself were ablaze.

The mass of humanity retreated to the river and the few bridges that were there. The edges of the river were choked with barges and other forms of riverboats. Unfortunately, many of them were made of wood or piled high with wood for the lumber mill located right on the river's edge. By midnight, the blaze had reached the Chicago River. Behind it, the city lay in a twisting, turning, churning mass of ashes, fire, debris, and collapsed buildings. Within those buildings lay men, women, and children while hundreds more pushed forward looking for some relief from the oppressive heat.

The downtown area lay ahead. The courthouse lay ahead. Some of the expensive homes owned by the richest in the city lay ahead. The firefighters, now from every corner of the metropolis, thought they would be able to prevent the fire from moving further and hoped to contain the already massive damage to the southern portion of the city. Then the docks, barges, and lumber along the river's edge burst into flames. The winds created by the out-of-control fire again sent embers high into the air where they were caught by more winds and those easily blew them across the southern branch of the Chicago River. The first major structure to catch fire was a church located just west of the river. Commercial coal yards along the river also began to burn. Each home had firewood stacked beside it. Soon, it seemed like nothing would stop this blaze.

The fire leaped the river and began to burn on the opposite shore. Now the city was truly in a panic. People began running for the lake. Others ran in whatever direction their feet would carry them. But they had few places to go.

The firefighters were completely unable to control the flames. The city government was now awake and the mayor was calling surrounding communities to bring in more firefighters, but it was obvious that the blaze was out of hand and that normal firefighting techniques were not going to work. As the fire continued north, driven as though by demonic force toward the heart of the city itself, it was obvious that Chicago was going to be lost. When the city's waterworks, located just north of the Chicago River, began to burn and stopped functioning, hopes of containing the blaze were completely lost. Evacuation was the only option left.

The streets became packed with fleeing families. Tales abound of families huddling under bridges and standing in rivers while the air around them turned blasting hot as embers fell around them. No rivers could hold the fire back as the embers flew high into the sky, catching roofs on fire even as firefighters battled putting out the burning houses and buildings behind them.

Nothing stood against the fire. As the flames touched the business district, the hotels, department stores, theaters, and printing facilities burned. Also burned were the opera house, churches, and more. The mansions along the north side of the Chicago River caught fire just like the poor tenements on the other side. The residents left their homes with the clothes on their backs and ran for the open areas of Lincoln Park and down by the lake. Others just did the best they could to stay ahead of the fire.

The flames eventually reached the City Hall. The prisoners in their cells began screaming for the police still in the building to let them out. The police and remaining firefighters battled the flames, but it was hopeless. Eventually, the building caught fire and the officers were forced to open the cells and let the prisoners run free. Then the officers themselves left, and no sooner was the building evacuated when the roof collapsed, the huge bell in the tower crashing through the tall steeple and into the basement of the building.

The fire pursued those who kept heading north. By 3 a.m. Monday morning, the Rumsey homes located on Huron Street were consumed by the inferno. At 3:30 a.m., the roof of the water pumping station collapsed and any attempts to effectively fight the fire at that point were over. The firefighters continued to try and fight the blaze, but their trucks were soon out of water and they could only stand by as the city burned around them.

Meanwhile, south of the city, the flames continued to burn. The brand new Palmer House burned and collapsed into a smoking pile of rubble. The offices of the newspaper the *Chicago Tribune* also burned to the ground. This was the same newspaper that had been fighting all summer long to improve the fire codes and conditions of the city. Soon, the buildings known as Terrace Row were burning and they became some of the last buildings south of the business district to burn.

On the north side, the wind continued to push the flames forward. By the middle of the day on Monday, the flames had reached North Avenue and eventually pushed to the northern-most limit of the city, at that time, Fullerton Avenue. Behind the flames was a shot from the center of Hell itself as the homes burned along with the streets, sidewalks, and everyone and everything in its path.

The crowds were everywhere. They stood and watched and listened at the Courthouse as it burned and the bell collapsed into the building. Those who worked in buildings downtown assumed that they were fireproof. Others thought, at first, that the fire would just be something eventually brought under control and ran to buildings to get higher views of the flames. Soon they found themselves surrounded by the flames as embers rained down upon them from the sky.

The bridges became clogged as the frantic families tried to escape the flames. Other families were separated as they tried to flee. Those in the rivers found that they too were not safe as the barges near the docks came loose and turned into flaming deathtraps. The rivers were also coated with grease which caught fire and turned the water itself deadly.

Reports began to surface of entire families trapped in their homes which then collapsed on top of them. Another rumor surfaced that a man was crushed by one of the bridges or beneath one of the Washington and LaSalle Street tunnels which had just opened earlier that year. Stories of heroism also surfaced along with tales of people who made narrow escapes from collapsing buildings and homes. Mixed with these were stories of looting or those who'd decided it was a good time to get drunk instead of fleeing. Some even charged money to help move carts and property.

To Survive the Flames

Survivors began to gather in areas of open prairie that existed to the west and northwest of the city at that time. They came in droves, their clothes smoking and their faces and skin covered with soot. They were burned and they were battered. They stood in dazed packs with lost looks and zombie-like stares. They stood and looked back and watched the flames leap high into the sky as the city continued to burn throughout Monday and into the second evening.

Because the fire had not discriminated, the prairies became a mixture of Chicago's rich and poor. The multi-millionaires who had fled their mansions mingled with the families of immigrants from small wooden shacks. They did their best to help each other, but there was little anyone could do.

A famous Union general, Philip Sheridan, helped coordinate some military help and relief. The mayor, meanwhile, placed the city under martial law. He placed Sheridan in charge of the relief efforts along with keeping the peace. Sheridan's home was spared the flames but his personal papers were consumed. Within a few days, martial law was lifted as the resources of the city were taxed to the limit.

By Tuesday, mother nature finally stepped in and helped out. The wind died down and then a light drizzle began. The rain actually began

began on Monday night, but continued into Tuesday. As the citizens stood in the rain, the water creating sooty streaks down their face, they watched the fires slowly diminishing and the rubble turn into smoking ruins. The heat from the fire was so intense that no one would be able to get close to the area of destruction for days even after the flames were out.

Once it was over, the fire had destroyed thirty-four blocks of the city. The entire length of the fire track was four miles. Throughout the entire event, the width of the path of flames was roughly three-quarters of a mile. Over seventy-three miles of wooden roads were destroyed as was 120 miles of wooden sidewalk. The property damage was in the neighborhood of $222 million. Of the 300,000 people who lived in Chicago, 90,000 were now homeless. Almost the entire area of what would be considered "downtown" Chicago was now a smoking ruin and there was pile after pile of rubble.

Recovery

Now the recovery period began. The first thing to do was to try and shift through the rubble for those who might have been buried there. During the first days after the fire, 125 bodies were pulled out from beneath buildings and homes. Today, most estimates of the dead range between 200 – 300 people. Considering the intensity of the fire and the population of the city, many consider this a very low number and a lucky break.

Rumors

It is true that the O'Leary house managed to survive the conflagration. The barn and the properties to the north were leveled and reduced to burning embers. The rumors began circulating almost as soon as the last of the burning buildings were put out. In fact, the first post-fire edition of the *Chicago Tribune* newspaper was already putting forth the story of Mrs. O'Leary and her cow. Given the times and the general hatred so many Americans had for the Irish, it was an easy story to sell and easier for those who had watched their homes burn to buy.

In truth, the entire story was a fabrication. Years later, the reporter, Michael Ahern, who had first written the story, retracted it. He declared that he had made the entire story up. Since then, the debate has raged over who really started the fire and how. No one knows for sure, although there are a few suspects.

One of them is Daniel "Pegleg" Sullivan who was the first person to report the fire. Sullivan told a convoluted story about being on a lawn near where the fire started and how he had seen flames in the O'Leary barn and then made some attempt to put them out. Some believe that Sullivan may have sneaked into the barn to try and steal milk and started a fire in some hay.

The problem with Sullivan's story and testimony after the fire lies within the layout of the O'Leary barn and where he said he was sitting. From that vantage point, he would not have been able to see the barn at all, must less a fire brewing inside the building. His stories of trying to put out the flames and rescuing any animals there was also suspect because he was not even singed. Despite his claims that he had run from the barn and up the street yelling the word "fire," none of the neighbors testified as having heard him despite the warm temperatures and the likelihood that their windows would have been open.

Another hypothesis is that Louis M. Cohn was in the barn playing craps. One theory says that he knocked over a lantern in an altercation with another player. One more rumor says that Mr. Cohn wrote down in his long-lost will that he had started the fire. One of the more interesting theories is that the fire was started by a meteor shower. This is because on the same night the Chicago fire started, another fire burned down the town of Peshtigo in Wisconsin which was 400 miles to the north of Chicago. Across the lake, the town of Holland, Michigan, caught fire and burned to the ground. The town of Manistee Michigan, just north of Holland, caught fire and burned while flames also destroyed Port Huron, Michigan. The theory goes that a meteor shower sent flaming rocks from the sky all across the entire area to cause the fires to all start the same night and at almost the same time. The Peshtigo fire and the fires in other Wisconsin towns actually killed between 1,200 to 2,500 people, but that fire is not known as well as the one that struck downtown Chicago.

No one knows for sure, of course. What *is* known is that, without the fire, the city of Chicago would probably not have become the city as it is known today. In fact, the rebuilding of the city began almost as soon as the last of the building fires were put out. The very first load of lumber for rebuilding arrived as the last of the buildings was extinguished.

Reform

The city began reforming the fire standards throughout the city almost immediately. In addition to removing the wood sidewalks and roads, the fire standards for buildings and the locations of things built were changed. Also changed were the standards and training for the fire department. Before too long Chicago had one of the finest fire fighting forces in the country.

Land speculators and developers descended upon the city and began rebuilding. Donations of clothes, food, and money began filling the city to help with the rebuilding. Before long, newer and taller buildings were going up where the burned-out downtown area used to be. Some of the first true skyscrapers began appearing and the neighborhoods of Chicago slowly rose again.

In just twenty years the city had developed to such an extent that it was decided to hold the World's Fair there. The Columbian Exposition was one of the most famous fairs of its kind and introduced the world to the "White City" as well as hot dogs and the Ferris Wheel. It showed the world that Chicago was back and a world-class city again.

The O'Learys never really did clear their names, unfortunately. To this day, most people assume that the cow in the barn and a careless Mrs. O'Leary started the fire. Their home stood on the property until 1956 when the remaining structures were torn down to build, of all things, the Chicago Fire Academy.

The Great Chicago Fire was, indeed, one of the worst fires to strike a major American city. It is probably the most famous fire, at the very least. Mixed with legend and speculation, the story has been taken as fact almost since the moment the last of the flames were extinguished. However, the city itself managed to come back stronger than ever. Not only did the city manage to do that, but it did so in a matter of two short decades which is remarkable when you consider what could have been the potential cost in property and human life.

Chapter Two

The Fireproof Theater

Throughout history, it has been proven that whenever someone declares a machine, place, or vehicle as the "best," it is a recipe for disaster. The people who built and then sailed the *Titanic* let the rumors that it was unsinkable sell tickets. There have been countless foolproof plans, indestructible buildings and vehicles, and almost all of them, one after another, have fallen apart, caught fire, crashed, or have been destroyed. So, it was probably only a matter of time before the Iroquois Theater in Chicago, which billed itself as "Absolutely Fireproof," was brought down in tragedy.

The Iroquois Theater was located at 24-28 West Randolph Street on the north side of the city. It was just between State and Dearborn Streets.

The theater had been open for only five weeks when the New Year's Eve shows sold out and the crowd began forming for the matinee. The theater had sent out the advertisements that it was fireproof shortly before it opened. The doors had opened for the first time on November 23rd and the biggest show of the season was going to be playing for the New Year's Eve crowd. What no one knew, however, was that the construction of the theater had been rushed to get the doors opened before Christmas. Therefore, some of the fireproofing that was intended to be in place was not and, in fact, some of the doors were not even operating.

The theater looked, to everyone else, as elegant as advertised. Marble and glass glittered throughout the elegant and extravagant lobby. The carpets that lead theater-goers to their seats were a deep and rich red. The banisters and other wooden accessories were mahogany. There was a six-foot ceiling in the promenade foyer. Marble staircases circled the entire theater, leading to the balconies. It was hailed in the local press and throughout the city and region as the latest in elegance, efficiency, safety, and convenience. Even though all of the fireproofing was not in place at the time the theater opened, it was hailed by everyone for the advances in that area and considered totally safe.

The seating for the theater could hold 1,600 comfortably. There was also room for standing-room-only and on the night of the tragedy about 100 of these tickets were sold. It was a show that was selling fast and extremely popular. It was a musical extravaganza called *Mr. Bluebeard* and starring the popular comedic actor Eddie Foy. The show had been promoted and hyped for weeks and was the perfect show for mothers to take their children on that December 30th as plans were made for further celebrations later that night to ring in the new year.

Foy himself would state later that he had never seen so many women and children at a show. The theater filled fast. The 1,600 seats were gone quickly and then the additional 100 standing-room spots began to fill in as well. People stood in aisles and in front of places that should have been exits. All of them were clamoring for the show to start and the play itself was filled with scenery of all kinds and what amounted to the state-of-the-art in special effects at the time.

Final Curtains

It was early afternoon and the curtain went up on the full house. The audience immediately lost itself in the music and action on the stage. Everything appeared to be going well and everyone seemed to be having a great time. Enthusiastic applause greeted the actors at the end of he first act.

As the curtain went up for the second act the eight men and eight women stepped out on stage for the first number. The song was called "In the Pale Moonlight" and it was accompanied by a powerful carbon light focused on a piece of scenery above the stage to create the illusion of moonlight. It was about 3:15 p.m. and things were about to turn from comedy and music into tragedy right in front of the audience.

The exact cause has never been determined. Some suggest it may have been a blown fuse. Some blamed the intensity of the lights. Some have said that one of the arc lights shorted. Whatever it was, a scorch mark about the size of a coin formed on one of the backdrops and was spotted by a stagehand. For several seconds it did nothing but blacken and then, suddenly, the tiny spot burst into flames. Above the stage, and just above where flames now were crawling, were nearly 300 backdrops waiting for their cues to drop down to the stage.

The actors and the audience didn't seem to notice. As the flames continued to crawl up toward the canvases above the stage, the flames began to cast an ethereal glow across the walls and curtains that were at the back of the stage. Most of the audience assumed this was part of the song and a special effect to keep the glow of the moon cascading down on the actors and the audience.

As the flames grew, the stagehand who had first seen the flames tried to beat out the flames using a broom. It didn't take long for the paint-covered canvases to burn out of control and well out of the reach of the stagehand. Within seconds, the entire top at the back of the stage was on fire and pieces of burning canvas began to slowly flit and float down to the floor.

The audience shifted in their seats nervously. Something about this just didn't seem like part of the show, but no one had told them that they were in any danger. As the actors continued to continue their show, the heat behind the stage began to grow and the flames began burning out of any attempt to control it.

There were fire extinguishers behind the stage but there were only six of them. As they were grabbed and turned on the fire, it became obvious that the flames had already grown out of control and the meager equipment was not going to stop it. Another stagehand stepped forward to lower a huge asbestos curtain from the top of the stage to separate the flames from the audience. The problem was that there was a wire from over the audience to the stage for a special effect for a flying fairy later in the play. The curtain got caught half-way down and couldn't seal off the fire from the people sitting in their seats.

Outside the theater, the weather had dropped to well below zero. The biting wind whirled around the building as, inside, the actors continued to perform. However, it soon became obvious that things were out of control. The dancers and singers on the stage for the start of the second act began to run. They headed for the large double-doors at the back of the stage which were used to move large pieces of scenery in and out of the theater. Once the cold air was let in, it served to only fan the flames and then blow them directly at the audience.

What happened next sent everyone into a panic. The influx of air created a massive fireball. Since the fire was up high, still above the stage, the fireball flew over the heads of those on the main floor still paralyzed in their seats. However, it turned the balconies and upper galleries into deathtraps. The fireball incinerated people sitting in those areas almost instantly, turning their clothing into flaming torches. Many were turned into cinders right where they sat, becoming fused to the seats around them.

Construction Flaws

Since the construction of the theater had been rushed for the holiday season, all of the ductwork was not complete. In fact, many of the air ducts were sealed. This created a chimney effect on the main floor of the theater, funneling the smoke and hot air straight up toward the ceiling of the main floor. The more doors and windows that the desperate audience opened to try and get out, the greater this effect became, causing more and more people to die from the flames.

On stage, the actors had attempted to keep going for as long as they could. Only when the flaming debris became too much did they rush for the back doors. The band tried to keep playing as well until the door opened and the fireball formed. With that, it became obvious to one and all that this was not part of the performance. The word "fire" was yelled throughout the theater. As the upper levels began to burn and the air became thick with smoke and the smell of burning clothing, tapestries, curtains, flesh, and hair, the crowd began to panic. It was then that the other problems with the construction of the theater became obvious.

The elegant marble and mahogany was meant to be on display for audience members to *ooh and ahh* over. What was not meant to be noticed were the fire exits scattered about the theater. As such, these exits were not marked and many were hidden behind thick curtains. As people rushed for the obvious exists, they became clogged in the doorways. Meanwhile, fire exits that could have led them to safety were missed entirely and never opened.

As if that weren't enough, the panicked and burning masses soon ran into problems with the working doors as well. It was a tradition at the time that the doors opened inward. As the mass of people began pressing against the doors it became impossible for those near the doors to get them open. As hundreds of men, women, and children pressed against them, it was impossible swing those doors inward. People began climbing on top of and over the masses who continued to press against the doors. Meanwhile the theater was catching fire all around them. The seats began to burn. The ceiling was on fire. The curtains on the stage were burned into tattered rags. The walls began to burn. The inside of the theater was like that of a giant oven and people began to literally bake where they stood.

The doors themselves had been made to be fashionable rather than practical. In addition to opening inward they were also equipped with locks common in Europe but new to people in America. It required lifting a lever before the door could be opened. As such, even those who were against the doors and had a chance to swing them inward, found themselves unable to open the locks in the panic and heat. One man recognized the kind of lock and managed to open a door while another door collapsed under sheer brute force of the weight of dozens of people behind it. Those, however, were the exceptions.

The air itself was on fire. As doors and windows were broken, each new influx of air caused more explosions and fireballs. People were collapsing, not from smoke inhalation, but because they were burning alive. Those caught at the back of the mass of humanity struggling to get through the doors were burned first and then the fire began to spread, jumping from clothing to clothing and hair to hair.

Help!

Backstage, most of the actors found themselves able to get out. Once the back door had been opened the flames back there had halted and were then blown toward the audience. They ran into the freezing cold air in various stages of undress and huddled against the theater for warmth.

The star of the show, Eddie Foy, stood on the stage for as long as he could. By all accounts, he tried to direct the evacuation as best he could from the stage. He attempted to the keep the audience calm, but eventually, the situation turned too dire. All around him pieces of scenery and the burning roof fell. It became too unbearable for him. He was nearly blind and choking from the smoke before he ran from the stage and out the stage door onto Dearborn Street.

Inside the hell that the theater had become, those who had decided they wanted to try and fight the fire found themselves unable to do anything. There was no fire alarm for them to pull. There were no fire buckets and no fire hoses. There were no fire extinguishers that anyone could find working. The ushers, much like the actors, had fled once the fire had started and didn't bother to stay behind to help anyone struggling.

While the flames and smoke were claiming many, there were those who died from things other than fire. Some fell as they were pushed and were trampled to death beneath a crush of bodies. Others, pressed against walls or up against doors that they had no hope of opening, found themselves crushed against a mass of people.

Some found themselves, especially in the upper levels, up against gates that had been locked and chained. Those who were on the upper levels and found themselves able to get out found that fire escapes had not been completed. They attempted to teeter on the ironworks that were there, but the crush of humans behind them pushed them forward, sending them plummeting into the alley below. Hundreds of bodies would be found later piled up outside the theater in the alleys from falling. Others were able to jump into the pile of bodies as they began to stack up and actually escape.

Across the street from the theater was Northwestern University. Several students saw the flames and the people climbing out of the building and crowding on the half-built fire escapes. Several of them grabbed ladders and tried to bridge the gap between the building for the university and the theater. They were not able to save many, but they did manage to save a few who bravely crawled across.

The firefighters finally arrived. They pushed their way through the front doors and made their way up the marble staircase. They immediately ran into a problem as they pushed on the doors and found that they were unable to open them. At first they thought it might have been the heat, but it soon became obvious that it was the sheer weight of bodies piled up on the other side that prevented the doors from swinging in. They threw their weight against the doors and moved to other areas of the theater where the bodies were not piled so high. They burst into a nightmare, but the fire itself was not nearly as bad as they thought. In fact, they had the fire under control and out entirely within twenty minutes. Then came the clean up.

The Cleanup

Those charged with cleaning out the theater had never seen anything like it. Charred corpses were piled between seven to ten feet high against the doors that wouldn't open. They found more piles of bodies around windows. Beneath those who had burned there were those who had suffocated beneath the crush of humanity. There were more who had suffocated from breathing the smoke and other gases.

Lying there in the theater were 575 people dead. There were hundreds more who were hurt. In the following weeks, thirty more people would die from their injuries. Of those who were on the stage or behind the stage, only one aerialist perished. Of those who worked for the theater, an usher and two female attendants died. The aerialist was meant to play a fairy who flew to the stage over the audience and got trapped above the stage when the fire broke out. The burns took her life days later. In one afternoon the death toll had doubled that of the Chicago Fire.

The fire was devastating but, like so many tragedies, it brought about huge changes for those who ran theaters. Fire codes that are in place to this day are directly because of this fire. The standing-room tickets in theaters were eliminated and the amount of people in a theater were limited to the amount of seats. Laws required that theaters be equipped with a proper number of working fire extinguishers and fire fighting equipment such as fire hoses. Sprinkler systems were also required in all theaters. Fire drills were to be held before performances with fire exits opened or pointed out by ushers. A fire proof curtain was required for stage and no flammable draperies were to be used. All scenery had to be tested for being fire proof. A fire guard was to be placed on stage at all times. Finally, all doors and exits had to open outward.

The tragedy at the Iroquois Theater was terrible considering the loss of life, but the one positive outcome is that you, in this day and age, can be safer in a theater.

Chapter Three

The Jazz Hotel

When you look at disasters, particularly those involving fire, one name seems to pop up again and again. For some reason, whenever a building was built with the name "LaSalle" attached to it, it seemed to be a recipe for disaster involving flame. There was a time, however, when Chicago was growing upwards rather than expanding outward. As skyscrapers were given birth within Chicago, they began to expand faster than the safety levels could keep up.

There were few hotels in the city that rivaled the Hotel LaSalle right in the heart of the downtown area. The hotel was twenty-two stories tall and located on the corners of La-Salle and Madison Streets. The hotel was finished being built in 1909 and was immediately promoted as the finest hotel in the city and one of the finest hotels outside of New York.

The architecture of the place was something to behold. The lobby was outfitted in marble and the decorations were ostentatious even by the early standards of the twentieth century. Everything about the place screamed opulence and wealth. Some of the biggest celebrities in the country and in the city stayed at the hotel.

In addition to being state-of-the-art when it came to architecture and amenities, the hotel also adopted a new style of management that had become popular at the time. The hotel had huge spacious rooms. The entire hotel was designed to cater to the wealthiest of travelers and vacationers. The accommodations were standardized for all rooms and all who stayed there. There were large, spacious public areas throughout the hotel. The range of services offered to those who stayed there was remarkable. There were bell-hops, a barber shop, restaurants with the finest foods and full-course meals, and the best in nighttime entertainment that the city could provide.

The Hotel LaSalle was interesting because there was a real effort attempting to cater to women as well as men. This was a relatively new trend in hotels around the country. Previous hotels offered smoking rooms and bars that catered specifically to men. However, now that the turn of the century had come, and women were stepping more and more out of the home, the hotels decided it was time to cater to them, too. So, out went all of the smoking rooms and in went beauty salons and stores that sold fine dresses and things appealing to women.

Within the luxurious Blue Fountain Room restaurant, the fine dining available there made a specific effort to entertain women. For example, Mrs. Potter Palmer, wife of the man who ran the Palmer House, was reported to be a regular customer.

The hotel's lobby echoed the decoration in the Blue Fountain Room. The walls were walnut panel and there was a rooftop garden. All of these things were meant to appeal to women just as much as men. In fact, the hotel had quite a number of prominent female guests throughout its time.

During the heyday of Chicago's jazz age, the hotel held a prominent role. It was still one of the finest hotels in the country. It competed well with the Palmer House and other hotels within the city of Chicago. It truly did compete with the hotels of the world as one of the finer places to stay in any city. The problem was that the fire standards of the world may have changed as time went on, but the Hotel LaSalle stayed as it was, which was, as you might have guessed, a disaster waiting to happen.

No Smoking Please

That disaster finally came on June 5, 1946. The hotel was still opulent and paneled with wood. The summer was hot and dry. It was night time when someone riding in one of the elevators did something very careless, thoughtless, and, ultimately deadly. Someone threw a cigarette down the Number Five elevator shaft. It was a small, simple thing, but it would soon lead to deadly consequences.

That lit cigarette caught something afire and the fire began to spread. Because the flames were in a chute, the elevator shaft, the column of air that ran up that shaft served to fuel the flames and they grew rapidly from a few embers into a full-blown conflagration that was soon burning out of control. Smoke began billowing up out of the shaft, filling each floor and then flames began shooting up through the elevator shaft and along the ceiling from the north elevator to the mezzanine. The flames eventually reached the seventh floor and then stopped.

Soon the cries of "Fire!" began to echo up and down the hallways.

There was no fire sprinkler system in place. There were very few fire-fighting methods available for anyone who wanted to help. There weren't even alarms to let those in their rooms know that there was real danger.

Those who heeded the calls and warnings found themselves pouring into hallways filled with thick black smoke. Guests began to inch their way down the halls and down the stairs. The air was filled with the sounds of people choking and gasping as they stumbled down the stairs.

Inside the rooms, however, there were those who were convinced that the calls about the fire were a joke. They stayed in their rooms, attempting to sleep as the choking smoke made its way under doors and between the cracks of the door. Many people died in their beds from asphyxiation.

Flames began to make their way down the halls. Other guests who went into the hallway and found themselves choking from the smoke headed back into their rooms. Escape routes were suddenly cut off and soon frantic guests were seen leaning out of windows and waving towels and handkerchiefs to get attention. Other guests wrote notes asking for help and threw them to the people crowding in the streets below.

The fire department and began to fight the fire. They tried to extend their ladders up to the eighth floor for the people who had been cut off by the flames that had reached to the seventh. It was then that they discovered their ladders couldn't extend that far. Some guests began jumping from the windows or hurled their luggage and furniture from their windows.

Other guests panicked while some reportedly remained very composed. There were stories of one woman calmly applying her make up as she leaned out of her eighteenth floor bathroom window awaiting rescue. Another woman was reportedly lead to safety by her seeing-eye dog. Spectators on the street ran into the hotel and helped other guests by dragging them out onto the street where they gasped at the fresh air, their faces covered with soot.

The firemen below began to enter the hotel, pouring water down the elevator shaft and fighting their way from the ground up. They found dozens of people cowering in their rooms, their bodies near the windows, choked from the smoke. Hardly anyone had died from the flames themselves. When the body count was totaled, there were sixty-one people found dead in one of the finest hotels in the world.

The Blame Game

The owners of the hotel were to take the blame. The city of Chicago immediately started an investigation and enacted laws that required hotels to increase the fire safety in their establishments. Escape routes were required for each room. Fire-fighting procedures for hotels were created. Automatic alarm systems were now required in all hotels throughout the city. Two-way radio devices were required by fire departments when fighting fires.

The owners, however, had been cited for fire-safety violations from as far back as 1927. At that time, they were warned about combustible draperies that the hotel had scattered throughout the building. The owners had never replaced those draperies.

The hotel itself was rebuilt and, amazingly enough, re-opened the following year. The Hotel LaSalle remained open, catering to guests, until the mid-70s, but never quite reached the magnificence it had attained during its hey-day. It was never quite the same.

Soon, other cities increased their hotel-safety regulations. Again, it took the deaths of far too many men and women to make changes throughout the country that would benefit the general public. The disaster had to happen in Chicago for the rest of the country to take notice.

Chapter Four

The Trolley

When you think of Chicago, there is a good chance you think of the famous EL which runs throughout downtown and, now, stretches to the suburbs both north, south, and west. It is hard to imagine the city without thinking of the streets with those steel struts supporting the tracks. It is hard not to imagine the roar of the trains as they run right past the windows of the office buildings that comprise downtown Chicago. Beneath these, on the streets, runs a comprehensive bus system that connects the various EL stops that you can't quite get to from one train to the other. All in all, Chicago has a very good public transportation system comprised of buses, subways, EL-trains, and commuter rails. However, it wasn't always the case.

At one time, like many cities throughout this country, the city of Chicago was connected through an extensive trolley system. Starting in 1859, these trolley lines snaked throughout downtown Chicago and into the surrounding areas carrying thousands upon thousands of passengers to work and shopping all around the city. At first, they were drawn by horses, but after the turn of the century, these trolley lines resembled the kind of vehicles you probably would think of. Tracks were run throughout the streets, and cars that looked a lot like buses were used with wires extending above the car to wires which ran along the streets. Passengers entered the cars from the street, paying their fares much like they do buses today and exited onto streets as well.

For much of the century, this served Chicago well. The problems involved were frustrating at times. For example, an accident in the road that stretched across the tracks made getting around those obstacles difficult for the trolleys attached to tracks and wires. If an accident occurred right in front of a trolley car it was impossible for the vehicle to swerve around it. If there was a flooded underpass, it was impossible to make a simple diversion so that the passengers and driver could move around.

By May 25, 1950, the trolley system was ingrained in the minds of most Chicagoans. While the city councilmen sometimes proposed the elimination of the trolleys in favor of a bus and subway system, in general, most people took the trolleys as a matter of course. The downtown area was still covered with wires and tracks and the cars criss-crossed the city carrying their precious cargo of men, women, and children.

In 1945 and 1946, the company that ran the trolley system, the Chicago Surface Lines, ordered a number of new cars from the St. Louis Car Company. The St. Louis Car Company had just introduced the new President's Conference Committee cars and they were sleek, smooth, quiet, quick to accelerate, and came in a mixture of cream and green paint schemes. They were quickly dubbed "Green Hornets" by the public.

The cars were created to be operated by two people. At the back of the car sat the conductor where three rear entrance door were located. It was his job to greet the passengers and collect the fares. The Green Hornets had the new "blinker" doors which slid sideways and resembled a blinking eyelid. The passengers entered at the rear and then exited the cars at the smaller middle doors or the larger blinker doors at the front of the car. At the front of the car sat the operator who was in charge of the speed and starting and stopping of the car.

The interiors of the cars were comfortable and modern for the time. The windows were cranked down much like in a automobile. They cranked down far enough that a very slim passenger, or maybe a child, could climb out the windows, but the company then added bars across the windows to prevent people from sticking their heads and limbs out and risk injury.

On May 25, 1950, the trolley with the designation of 7078 was assigned to the Broadway-State route. This was a particularly long route that ran all the way from Devon Avenue on the north side to 119th Street on the far south side. The night before this fateful day, a rainstorm had drenched the city. This had resulted in several viaducts becoming flooded which would require that the street cars would have to be diverted using elaborate re-routing methods. Since each car ran on electricity and ran low to the ground, it was impossible for them to just travel through the flooded viaducts.

One of the routes that would be affected by this was the route for trolley 7078. What would soon happen was a huge list of mistakes and confusing rules that caused one of the largest motor vehicle accidents in United States history and changed the way public transportation would exist in the Windy City from that point forward.

Before 7078 approached the flooded viaduct, a previous streetcar had been told to stop, go back, and then divert to a switch track that would allow the driver and the passengers to go around the flooded area. It was a difficult operation and it slowed down the lines in general and backed up traffic. The flooded area was also causing problems with traffic as cars and trucks slowly crawled through the water. When the previous street car had made the turn, the switch was left open for reasons no one was ever able to determine. Because everything was running late, the driver of car 7078 was driving faster than he should have been.

Stationed near the viaduct was a man with a flag. He waved the cars to a stop and then guided them back to the turnaround portion where the elaborate detour could occur. He had been diverting traffic and the trolleys all morning long. Trolley 7078 was in working order and it had been recently checked. The car was also moderately full, as most of the cars were that morning, taking people to work.

Circumstances coming the other direction seemed to be making things much worse. A gasoline truck driven by a man named Mel Wilson was headed northbound. The truck was headed for gas stations in the neighborhood and had almost 8,000 gallons in the tank. It too was approaching the flooded viaduct at a high rate of speed.

No one has ever been sure exactly how the motorman running car 7078 missed the man with the flag. It has been theorized that the man ignored him. How he could not have known about the flooded viaduct and the turnaround also remains a mystery. What *is* known is that the trolley came into view moving fast and the flag man began waving his flag frantically. The flagman stood there in shock as the trolley shot past him and then hit the open switch from where the prior streetcar had made its turnaround.

The trolley struck the open switch and immediately jumped its rails. It then veered into the northbound lane. The passengers inside were thrown against first one side, and then the other, and were sent into screaming piles of people. There may have been just a moment when the motorman and Mel Wilson, the truck driver, saw each other and then the two vehicles collided near an intersection. There was a hideous sound of crunching metal, breaking glass, screeching brakes, and people screaming. Then, as the impact shot along the street, a spark was struck and 8,000 gallons of gasoline exploded into flames. Just before the gas truck exploded, the trolley had torn open the hull of the tank and sent a flood of gasoline into the street, which now became a river of fire. As stunned witnesses stood by looking on in terror, they saw a single fireball erupt from the tanker and completely engulf the trolley.

The trolley had been full. Every seat was taken and the sudden turn had sent them tumbling into the aisle. As the fireball erupted they found themselves trapped inside the green and cream vehicle as the world turned to flame outside. Those that had time to get to their feet found themselves baking alive as the flames covered the outside of the trolley, turning metal white hot and then setting the interior on fire. Those inside began to pile up against the side doors and the rear doors. They found that those doors would not open.

The windows were designed to be aesthetic rather than as escape routes. Those who tried to climb out found that the windows only rolled down so far and even if they could wedge an arm out, they could climb no further because the bars across the bottom of the windows prevented them from crawling out. Inside, the heat reached extreme levels. The clothing, hair, and flesh were melding into one giant mass from the heat and the screams from inside were only partially drowned out by the sound of the flames from the fire that covered the trolley.

Somehow thirty passengers managed to crawl out of the wreck. Even those who managed to survive were severely burned. Behind them, thirty-three other passengers were burned alive, trapped against the doors. After the accident, it was revealed that one fourteen-year-old girl had been quick enough on her feet to locate and pull a knob that would open the center doors. This allowed many of those who survived with severe burns to get away.

The explosion itself rocked the entire neighborhood. Windows shattered up and down the street and buildings shook. The fireball itself shot two to three stories into the air. Because of the ripped sides of the gas truck the flames rocketed down the street and lit up seven buildings along State Street. The walls of some of those buildings collapsed after the shock of the explosion and then the heat from the flames. The heat was so intense that metal melted and twisted, glass from surrounding buildings was fused and parts of the street were melted as the asphalt grew too hot.

The fire alarms began to ring. Thirty fire companies responded and arrived upon a scene of horror. They began pouring water on the out-of-control fire and it would take nearly two hours for them to get it back under control. Meanwhile, as many as 20,000 people came out of their homes and offices to watch the fire and the flames. The smell of burning flesh hung in the air and would linger in the area for days after the accident.

Once the fire was out, the horror show really began. The emergency workers who arrived were scarred by the sights that greeted them. They pried the doors, smoke billowing from inside the vehicle and the smell of burnt hair, clothing, and flesh hanging thickly around their noses and mouths. They worked and worked to pry open the rear doors and what greeted them was a pile of black and burned flesh that did not resemble humanity anymore.

According to some reports, they were not even able to find body parts in some instances. They found skulls and parts of limbs. All of them had to be removed and placed nearby in a temporary morgue. They discovered that the other doors had no emergency lever that could have been pulled. The passengers had bottlenecked at the doors and been fused together by the intense heat.

Once the wreckage was pulled away from the scene, investigators set about pulling it apart and inspecting it. It was quickly determined that car 7078 was in perfect working order. They also determined that the gasoline truck was also working just fine. Both the motorman and the driver of the truck had been killed in the accident, so interviewing them was impossible. Most of the fingers pointed to the driver of the trolley who had had ten minor accidents before this one.

The real blame fell on the construction of the trolley car itself. The problems cited included the lack of emergency pull levers throughout the car so that the doors could be opened in case of an accident. The steel bars across the windows prevented anyone who could open the windows from escaping. The doors of the vehicle, other than the small side doors with the emergency escape lever, could not be opened by anyone outside or inside the car. It was a senseless tragedy that cost thirty-three people their lives.

Those who had been pushing for the elimination of the trolley system suddenly found themselves in the majority. The public itself seemed shocked by the tragedy and the neighborhood where the accident occurred took months to recover. The trolleys began to slowly disappear from the streets of Chicago along with the tracks and the wires overhead.

Eventually, a comprehensive bus system was put into place and the Chicago Transit Authority took over the public transportation duties for the city. These days, there are no tracks left in the streets to remind those who live in Chicago that trolleys once criss-crossed the entire area. Meanwhile, the bus system has expanded past the borders of the city of Chicago and into the suburbs with the creation of the Regional Transportation Authority.

Chapter Five

The School Fire Among the Angels

The Our Lady of Angels Elementary School held classes for children from kindergarten through eighth grade. It was located at 909 N. Avers Avenue in an area known as Humboldt Park on the west side of the city. It was a Catholic school run by the Chicago Roman Catholic Archdiocese. On December 1, 1958, the school was the educational home of about 1,600 children. The school building itself was a two-story stone structure with wooden stairways and interiors. It was constructed in 1910 and had been expanded and remodeled numerous times by the time 1958 arrived. The building was also in total compliance with the existing fire codes of that time, but the weaknesses in those codes would become tragically clear on this fateful day.

Much of the block was taken up by a full complex at the location where the school was located. In addition to the school, there was a church and a rectory which was adjacent to the Sisters of Charity of the Blessed Virgin Mary convent and church.

The problems within the school became evident once the tragedy was over. The door to each classroom had a glass transom above it which could be opened to let in air for ventilation purposes. This was fine to cool the rooms but would also allow flames or smoke to enter the rooms unabated. The school only had one fire escape and no automatic fire alarm. There was no direct alarm to the local fire department. The stairwells were not fire proof and there were no fire doors to block flames in the stairwell. There were no heat detectors, and in that era, the idea of overhead fire sprinklers were thought of as things for factories or new schools. Anything resembling a modern smoke detector did not exist at that time. The interior of the school was built almost entirely of wood. The walls, floors, doors and even the roof had wood. The second floor had twelve-foot ceilings and the windows from that floor were twenty-five feet off the ground which would be intimidating for anyone wanting to jump. There were only four fire extinguishers in the building and they were mounted seven feet off the ground.

Smoldering into Flames

Since it was December in Chicago that meant the air was cold on the day the greatest school fire tragedy in the history of this country occurred. The fire itself began, according to most thoughts and investigators, about 2 p.m. The school was set to be dismissed at 3 p.m. The fire began in a cardboard trash can located in a stairwell. It is believed that the fire burned unnoticed for about ten to thirty minutes in the trash can. A thin line of gray smoke slowly began to billow from the trash can into the stairwell. The can itself caught fire and began heating the air within the stairwell.

On the first floor there was a thick wooden door at both ends of the long hallway. This prevented much of the smoke and the fire from spreading to the floor. Due to open windows and doorways, a steady breeze was blowing through the stairwell which made the entire stairway like a giant chimney. It funneled smoke, hot gas, and flames upward toward the second floor. Once it reached the second floor there was nothing there to stop it. There was no thick door. There were doors with windows that could be opened and, in fact, in the stairwell where the flames were growing, the window at that end was open, letting smoke and fire reach the second floor unabated.

The fire was left to burn for a long time before anyone noticed. The stairwell brought the heat to unimaginable levels. The heat caused windows to crack and then break, which let in more air and caused the flames to spread higher and higher. By the time 2:25 p.m. arrived, three girls returning from an errand that brought them near the stairwell filled with smoke, began coughing, the thick black smoke tearing their eyes. They ran to room 211 and entered via a back door and told their teacher, Sister Helaine O'Neill, who had not noticed or smelled the smoke.

Sister O'Neill began lining up her students at the door of the classroom. She planned on heading out of the building to safety. Sister O'Neill stood at the front of the line and then opened the classroom door. She immediately encountered the thick smoke. It was so thick she couldn't see and she couldn't breathe. Both she and the students began coughing and gagging against the smoke. She deemed it was too dangerous for them to leave, so she herded the students back into the classroom and told them to take their seats. It would be several more minutes before the fire alarm was pulled.

The heat in the stairwell caused a window to shatter. The fire, which had been smoldering and building in intensity, blew into a full-blown conflagration now. The wooden staircase was the next thing to go as the flames leaped from the garbage can into the air. The stairwell completely filled with smoke, hot gases, and flames, turning it into an inferno.

Fire Department Woes

The school's janitor, James Raymond, happened to be walking past the school on the outside. A glow caught his eye from the area of the stairwell. He ran into the school and ran down to the basement where he peered through a window. He looked into a scene right out of hell. He warned two young boys who were walking past that they should get out of the building and then ran next door to the rectory. He told several people there that there was a fire at the school and they should call the fire department. As of now, the school's fire alarm still had yet to be pulled. Raymond ran back to the school and began assisting with evacuation via a fire escape.

The two boys ran back to their classroom and informed their teacher that there was a fire. That teacher, in turn, contacted another teacher and the two of them tried frantically to find the principal to get permission to evacuate. They couldn't locate the principal so they decided to evacuate their classrooms under their own authority. They lined up the children and began leading them out of the building. One of the teachers found the fire alarm and pulled the lever, but the alarm didn't sound. She returned to her children and continued leading them out of the building. They grouped their students in the church and then the one of the teachers returned to the building and pulled the fire alarm for a second time. This time the alarms sounded, but they did not have a direct connection to the fire department; the alarms just sounded within the building.

Things were going from bad to worse on the second floor. The smoke was now billowing through the halls. The open transoms on the classroom doors were allowing the smoke to billow into the classrooms and fill the young lungs and the lungs of the nuns with smoke. The nuns and the students knew that there was danger now, but it had been burning so long, their escape routes were suddenly being cut off.

Still, the fire department had not been called. Even though the janitor had gone into the rectory and announced that there was a fire and that someone needed to call the fire department, they had yet to be called. The first call was finally put into the department at 2:42 p.m., nearly forty-five minutes after the fire had started, the fire department was finally contacted. Not long after that first call, a second was made by a woman who ran a candy store directly across the street from the school. The fire was burning out of control in the stairwell. Open windows in stairwells around the school were fanning the flames. Open doors were also feeding oxygen into the fire, causing it to spread faster. Now a construction element of the building itself would make things worse.

A pipe chase ran from the basement to the cockloft which was just above the second floor. There was a lowered ceiling for the second floor and the space between the ceiling and the roof was the perfect place for heat and smoke to start gathering and create another dangerous and deadly concern. What was, essentially, an attic began to heat up and continued to heat up until it reached ignition point and then burst into flames. The pipe chase funneled the heat and the flames into that space above the second floor and caused it to burst into flames. Fire swept down ventilation grates into the second floor corridor and then flashed through the cockloft directly above the classrooms. Those glass transoms above the doors to each of the classrooms cracked and then burst into shards. Now flames began entering the classrooms along with walls of smoke.

Prayers

While the second floor had become a living hell, the first floor was quietly and quickly evacuated. By the time those nuns and students left on the second floor realized just how much danger they were in, the hallway outside the classrooms was filled with smoke and flames blocking their only exit. The only way to reach fresh air was to crawl out onto a tiny ledge outside their second-floor windows and jump the twenty-five feet to the cold hard concrete below. The other option was to sit back down in their seats and begin to pray. Some of the nuns did exactly that, upon studying the windows and the fall awaiting them. Several gathered the desks into semi-circles and encouraged the children to pray.

Eventually, the smoke heat and flames would get to all of them, even those praying, and they would be forced to flee toward the windows. When they got there and found that no firemen were waiting for them with nets and fire trucks, they began to jump. Some were pushed as they climbed up into the windows by those scrambling for safety behind them. Others simply fell as they tried to find a way to stand in the windows and gasp for air.

The firemen had actually arrived at the huge church and school location four minutes after being called. However, they had been given the wrong address and ended up at the rectory instead of the school. This cost them critical minutes as the trucks were driven back around and repositioned to battle the blazing school. By the time they arrived, they were greeted with a nightmare. Children clung to the windows, their white shirts turning brown and then black. Those still trapped in the classrooms were coughing and gasping and even burning. The entire structure was becoming unstable as the wood in the ceilings, floors, and stairs burned away to ash. Smoke billowed out of the available windows and spaces and sent a giant plume of smoke into the Chicago sky.

The firefighters tried to get to the children as fast as they could, but they kept running into obstacles. As they tried to run toward the north wing, which overlooked a small courtyard, they ran into a locked gate. It was routine for those gates to be locked, but now the firemen couldn't get to the children in the windows. They spent minutes hammering at the metal gates with sledgehammers and a ladder before they were able to break through.

Horror Scenes

The conditions in the classrooms were getting worse. As the firemen reached the windows, they peered into a sight that would haunt many of them for the rest of their lives. Inside the classrooms children were running everywhere they could to try and get out of reach of the choking smoke and intense heat. Others were clawing and scratching at each other to get to the windows. Some of the younger or smaller of the children were pushed out of the windows by the children behind them even as ladders were reaching the spot. Firemen reported seeing children jumping blindly, their hair and clothing on fire. Many fell to their deaths. Others were pulled back into the burning rooms by those grabbing them from behind. As the firefighters reached the windows with their ladders and began pulling the children out of the windows, the rooms began to literally explode in flames and then portions of the ceiling began to collapse.

Word of the fire began to spread throughout the city. Local television and radio stations began covering the fire and the activity. Frantic parents left their jobs and hysterical mothers fled into the streets and began crowding around the area, screaming for their children and crowding police and firemen.

All around the school, neighbors began trying to help. The woman who owned the candy store across the street brought students into her store and into the home she had behind the store. Other neighbors, seeing the smoke, ran to the building with ladders that turned out to be woefully short to reach the windows and those clinging to the ledges. An elderly neighbor actually suffered a stroke while trying to help children away from the school. Others ran to the scene with blankets as children with no coats sat shivering in the cold December air. Still others opened their doors, providing warm shelter, warm liquids to drink and food.

Inside the school, one nun rescued two children by rolling them down a flight of stairs after they had frozen at the top in fear. Other nuns ran into the school, helping children fight their way through the smoke and flames. Ambulances began arriving along with the firefighters and five different area hospitals became the sight for the burned and injured. Priests from the rectory ran into the flames and also guided choking and smoke-blind students to the doors. One of the priests actually was able to pass students through a window, across a small courtyard, to a window in the second floor annex.

The coverage of the fire electrified the city. More and more parents began leaving work, or their homes. Soon, the streets around the school were choked with hundreds of parents, pushing against the police who were trying their best to keep the area clear. Above the scene a helicopter containing a Chicago police officer sent regular reports to a local radio station, providing on-the-scene coverage. Frightened mothers pleaded with the police to be let into the school and were told they would have to wait as the fire slowly diminished and the sad task of removing the bodies began to happen.

As the fire ended and the charred and broken school rooms were searched, the grim task and the depth of the tragedy soon became apparent. On the day of the fire, eighty-seven students and three nuns lay dead beneath the wreckage. Just before Christmas, three more severely burned and injured children died and then two more just after 1959 rang in. One more child held on until August of 1959, before succumbing to wounds suffered during the tragedy. In the end, ninety-two children and three nuns were dead totalling of ninety-five deaths in one afternoon.

In the school, the firefighters reported scenes of total destruction that would haunt them for the rest of their lives. They told of moving timber and beams and finding tiny charred bodies that then crumbled and fell apart in their hands as they attempted to lift them out of the carnage. As parents watched stretcher after stretcher coming out of the school, the cries of fear turned into cries of despair.

The tragedy received national coverage in the media. Many throughout the country interrupted their normal broadcasting to turn to live coverage of the event. The newspapers and local news was filled with images of tiny coffins, all of them brilliantly white, lined up in morgues. Then came the funerals, one after another, as each tiny casket was carried, presided over, and then carried again to be planted in the ground. Once again, Chicago was crying, but the new surge in national news coverage allowed the rest of the country to weep along with them.

Investigators set about probing the wreckage and trying to find a reason for the fire. To this day, no actual cause has ever been given. In 1962, a young man, a fifth grader, confessed to setting the fire but then recanted his confession. He also confessed to police to setting fires throughout his neighborhood including several in apartment buildings. During the day of the fire, he had been excused from his classroom at around 2 p.m. to go to the restroom which would have put him potentially in the area where the fire started at the time investigators believed the first flames licked against the garbage can. Fire investigators also said they found burned matches in an undamaged area in a chapel located in the basement of the north wing.

The boy was taken seriously at the time and questions intensely by police and fire investigators. He was even hooked up to a lie-detector. During his confession he did provide details about the location of the fire that had not been made public and he probably should not have known. However, he was not prosecuted as the evidence linking him to the scene just wasn't there.

Safety and Mourning

As for the school itself, it was considered as safe as it could be for the time. Standards of fire safety for schools were different up until the time of the fire. The school had undergone a safety inspection just a few weeks before the fire and it had passed. Although it did not match all of the fire standards in place for 1958, it had been grandfathered in with the standards it did meet as part of the new safety standards implemented in 1949. At that time, those who did not match the newer standards were not required to retrofit their schools to match the new standards.

As the city mourned, the country responded. A relief fund was created to help families who had lost children or to care for children injured. Even Hollywood responded with the likes of Jack Benny visiting the injured in local hospitals. The flags across the city were lowered, by order of the mayor, to half-mast. Even Pope John XXIII responded by sending a telegram to the Archbishop of the Chicago Catholic Diocese. As the Archbishop and the mayor toured the school and then visited the hospitals and morgues they were both profoundly shaken and the mayor began to demand higher safety standards in local schools.

Life magazine ran a story about the fire. In that story, a famous picture by Steve Lasker showed a firefighter named Richard Scheidt carrying the badly burned and soot-covered body of ten-year-old John

Michael Jajkowski, Jr. from the building. This image later became a famous fire-prevention safety poster used around the country. The little boy had succumbed to the smoke like many of the others.

The tragedy did bring about changes across the country and made schools safer for children everywhere. The president of the National Fire Protection Association stated that changes would be made in the school fire safety regulations. Those buildings that had not met current standards were now required to bring themselves up to current codes. This affected 16,500 older school buildings. Chicago's fire codes and new amendments to the Illinois state fire codes were also passed. The number of fire-drills were increased, fire standards within the schools, improved materials for buildings, fire extinguishers, alarms connected to fire stations, and improved fire doors were implemented. Fire safety investigators from around the world, some as far away as London, made the trip to Chicago to see what could be learned and to make changes to their own school safety codes.

The school was rebuilt. The new school was built at a different location, on Iowa Street, and opened again to students in 1960. The school was up to code to the latest regulations and beyond and even had a state-of-the-art overhead sprinkler system. The new Our Lady of Angels continued to teach students until the 1990s when declining numbers of students forced the Archdiocese of Chicago, after the Class of 1999 graduated, to close. The building is now being used at this writing by the Galapagos Charter School.

Once again, Chicago had suffered a great tragedy. The saddest part of this tale was that those who paid the price for progress were dozens of children. The entire nation looked on in surprise as fire swept through a Chicago landmark and claimed the lives of these young victims.

However, as with many tragedies this profound, it brought about changes that improved the lives of children in schools around the world. It made people stop and realize that the schools they sent their children to every day may not always be the safest place. It made those who ran those schools understand the importance of staying up to code and ensuring the safety of the children they cared for and taught. Once again, Chicago led the way, with profound disaster.

Chapter Six

Finally
Learning from the Past

If Chicago were to have a problem that kept repeating itself when it came to fires, it would have to be allowing older buildings to maintain their outdated fire safety when the fires safety regulations changed. Time and again it seems that the various officials who were in charge of taking care of the public just let the older buildings go on as if nothing had changed. This proved to be a fatal mistake.

The entire city of Chicago sits in the County of Cook. It is one of the largest and most populated in the entire state of Illinois. It takes a huge amount of government and government administrators to keep things running. Their headquarters are located in downtown Chicago, in a huge, old building known simply as the Cook County Administration Building on Washington Street. It has the same unique architecture that so many downtown Chicago buildings have when they were built a long time ago. Like many of those older skyscrapers, it had failed to keep up with modern fire safety standards, despite the fact it was actually a government building.

Cook County Administration Building

On October 17, 2003, as the hundreds of employees within that building were working, a small fired started in a supply closet on the 12th floor. It was a very small fire. In a modern building, set to proper modern fire codes, it would have been an insignificant and easily maintained fire. However, in the Cook County Administration Building this fire had several things working in its favor, but working against the employees.

In Favor....or Not

The first thing was that the supply closet was located right next to one of the two major stairwells that employees were supposed to use to evacuate in case of an emergency. It was so close that any fire and smoke would likely be sucked right into that stairwell, filling the stairs and the space around those trying to evacuate with thick black, choking smoke. Employees trying to walk in an orderly way would soon find themselves encased in smoke, blinded, choking, and likely panicking.

The second thing working in the fire's favor was that the stairwells did not have modern fire doors. When someone entered the stairwell and the doors closed behind them, those in the stairwell would find themselves locked *in* that stairwell. Their only choice would be to go all the way down to the bottom. Of course, if they were above the fire and running into that smoke, doing so would become impossible. This would leave workers trapped in a space rapidly running out of breathable air. Most modern buildings have "smart locks" which trigger when an emergency is called and the alarms pulled.

Third, the stairwells were old and outdated in another way. Most modern buildings use pressure in the stairwells that keeps the doors shut in case of an emergency and provides a barrier of air against any fires that might be burning in the hallways. The building lacked these pressurized stairwells which would allow the smoke to freely enter the stairwell unabated.

The fourth thing the fire had working for it was outdated and incorrect procedures within the building for proper evacuation. Most high-rise buildings do not require employees located *above* smaller fires to evacuate. In fact, as mentioned earlier, this is generally a bad idea because those coming *down* the stairs from above during a fire are likely to run into the smoke and flames. Unless the building integrity itself is in danger, it is usually better for those above the fires to stay where they are and let firefighters and building fire suppression systems deal with the problem. This procedure was not in place in the administration building.

Fifth, the building did not have sprinklers on every floor. Built before the mentioned codes had been put into place, the building was never required to comply with the newer regulations. Therefore, the building had sprinklers in the lobby, but not above it. Thus, the small fire would easily become a larger, more dangerous fire very quickly with little to stop it.

Finally, the city of Chicago had not yet instituted all of the necessary preparations needed to coordinate police and fire departments in case of a high-rise emergency. Despite September 11, 2001 being the wake-up call for cities around the world to make sure such procedures were in place, Chicago had not yet created a standard. The police and fire departments used different radios and even broadcast and communicated on different frequencies that varied by station and department. Therefore, as the fire grew, and more and more fire departments and police officers from around the city joined in to help look for both the fire and workers trapped inside, they were unable to coordinate search efforts effectively.

All of these things combined would lead to tragedy for six employees within the Administration building. It would be nearly fatal for thirteen, but herculean efforts by firemen and paramedics would reduce that number greatly.

Evacuations

The fire began small and went unnoticed for some time. Soon, however, the fire had spread within the supply closet and smoke found its way out of the room and began pouring down the stairwell. Eventually, the smoke was spotted and a fire alarm pulled. The fire department was called. Building management made its first mistake by requiring that the entire building, including floors above the fire, be evacuated.

By all accounts, employees followed the fire evacuation procedures they had been taught. They followed each other to one of the two stairwells that they were supposed to use in case of a fire. Floor after floor of office workers left their offices and cubicles and began walking down the stairs. One employee, realizing that the doors would lock behind them, on the 27th floor, used a doorstop to prop the doors open. This would turn out to be a life-saving action for many.

The firefighters arrived quickly, and soon assessed where the fire was coming from. They even quickly made their way to the 12th floor and found the fire. However, they soon broke down the door into the stairwell to get at the fire. The smoke, which had been trickling into the stairwell, now had nothing to stop it. The enclosed stairwell was now filling rapidly with smoke. The stairwell itself acted like a kind of giant chimney.

Employees heading down that stairwell soon found the going impossible. Many decided to turn around and head back up the way they had come. This is when many also found that they were unable to open the doors from the stairwells. This started a kind of panic as the air became thicker and thicker with smoke. Many continued to go up rather than down, hoping to find some kind of relief. Employees who reached the 27th floor found the door propped open and ran for safety.

For at least thirteen employees, however, reaching the 27th floor proved impossible. As firefighters got the fire under control, they began searching. They found the bodies of these employees, all of them collapsed in the stairwell that was filled with smoke. Firefighters dragged them out of the smoke and managed to revive seven. Six employee didn't make it.

More Regulations

Chicago had learned a hard lesson. An inquiry was held and, in 2004, new safety standards were enacted. One of the first was the creation of a High-Rise Incident Command Officer for any high-rise fire. This one person would coordinate and organize the efforts of all the emergency responders. Hopefully, this would better organize the search and rescue efforts in the future.

Next, it became official policy that searches of all stairwells from top to bottom were mandatory. This had not been the case when the fire was reported. Combined with the communication problems, this led firefighters to not search the stairwells as thoroughly as they should have.

The communication issues were addressed. There had been problems with the firefighters communicating and many had ended up just contacting 911. Operators for 911 then attempted to contact those fighting the fires and responders in the field to locate those in trouble. As more reports came from within the building, the mixed traffic of civilians and emergency workers trying to communicate quickly overloaded the 911 system.

The city of Chicago also announced a partnership with the Illinois Fire Service Institute. More training was needed by city firefighters to deal with high-rise and skyscraper incidents such as this. This training would better prepare firefighters for any future problems or emergencies of any kind in the huge buildings that comprise downtown Chicago.

Once these new policies were accepted, it was hoped, by all across the city, that it would be a very long time before they were tested. Sadly, this was not to be. On December 6, 2004, the city and its firefighters would be tested in a cold Chicago winter as more employees in a high-rise office building in downtown Chicago attempted to survive an office fire.

The LaSalle Bank Building

This time, the building was the LaSalle Bank Building located right in the Loop, or heart, of downtown Chicago. Once again, the name "LaSalle" seemed to prove a curse. It was faulty wiring that would cause this fire, and this time, the fire would burn for more than five hours when it broke out on the 29th floor. The heat from those flames would reach an excess of 2,000 degrees and eventually reach up to the 30th floor.

This fire would turn out to be the biggest high-rise fire in Illinois history. Before the flames were out and the building evacuated, over 400 firefighters would respond. Nearly one-third of the apparatus used by the Chicago Fire Department would be used to fight the blaze. Twenty-five suburban communities would lend a hand and send fire support to combat the fire and see to rescue operations. The scene was set for this to be a tragedy easily surpassing that of the Cook County Administration Building.

However, the fire departments had learned from the previous fire. First, they found that the very design of the building lent itself to a better method of fighting the fires. The building was tiered which allowed firemen to set up and fight the fire from the various tiered rooftops. Some of the firemen were just a few floors below the flames on the 29th floor and were able to pour water onto the windows of that floor.

The new policies enacted because of the Cook County Administration Building fire were put into effect. A single person was put in charge of communications and coordination, even between the suburban fire departments. Rapid Ascent Teams, who had spent so much time training with Illinois Fire Service Institute, were sent into the building to start the evacuation and fire-fighting procedures. They began searching all of the stairwells and staircases.

The fire was reported well after the normal times when the bank would be open. At the same time, it was determined that that there were 500 employees still in the building. The firefighters declared one stairwell as the official evacuation stairwell. The second stairwell was designate for use by the firemen. At the same time, the 911 operators were in constant contact with those in the building and helped keep them calm and orderly. They were also contacting the firefighters to guide them to where there were trapped employees.

Meanwhile, the doorways to the stairwells were kept unlocked so that employees could access the floors as needed. The PA system gave clear instructions to the employees about who should and should not evacuate. The building had also been undergoing frequent fire drills to make sure the employees knew where to go and what to do.

The firefighters were able to put out the fire and help the 500 employees still inside evacuate. Although there were over thirty injuries, most of them were firefighters and not workers. Some were treated for smoke inhalation and minor injuries. Despite this, there was not a single death throughout the entire incident.

The city had, at last, learned its lesson. They had enacted rules that required high-rise buildings and the people in them to know what to do during an emergency. This prevented the panic that had occurred in the previous fire. The workers had remained calm and did what they were instructed.

At the sane time, the fire department had taken their lessons to heart. The training they had received proved effective as did the communications improvements. The various departments were able to communicate and find those who needed help.

It had taken a tragedy the year before for the city to realize there were deficiencies. However, once those lessons had been learned, it turned out the new rules were effective. Now, Chicago was ready should any kind of emergency hit one of the buildings downtown.

Part Two
City of Water

Chicago has always been a transportation hub. For those who know a bit about history, they probably know that Chicago was once the railroad center of the entire country. It was said that all rail-lines lead to Chicago—and that wasn't an exaggeration. Others who may *not* know history that far back, may at least know that modern Chicago is the home of O'Hare International Airport—one of the busiest airports in the world. What many probably don't know is that before there were railroads, there were ships and Chicago was a major shipping center and transportation center in those days of water travel.

At one time, if you looked out upon Lake Michigan, you would have seen boats almost as far as the eye could see. Schooners with sails and masts criss-crossed each other. These were joined by barges, tugs, and cargo ships. People traveled via boat across the lakes. The Chicago River and surrounding tributaries were filled with more boats and ships carrying people and cargo to all areas of the country.

Situated right near the tip of Lake Michigan, the city was born to be a port. It is nevertheless important in some respects in this way, but not compared to what it once was. These days, the boats are likely to be there more for pleasure than commerce. Still, even in modern times, Chicago is a city of water.

Chapter Seven

The Christmas Tree Ship

It was November in Chicago and the Christmas season was starting to spread its cheer throughout the city. The year was 1912 and, back in those days when people put Christmas trees in their homes, they used real trees. Since those trees didn't grow in the city, they had to be transported via train or boat from other states. This is where the ship called the *Rouse Simmons* came into play during those days. The ship itself had become legendary as part of the holiday season when it would pull up at the docks and unload its cargo of Christmas trees.

The ship was helmed by a man named Herman Schunemann who had a gruff exterior that you would normally associate with a man who captained a ship in the rough waters of the Great Lakes. However, he was also known as Santa Claus to dozens of children and families every Christmas season. Schunemann spent the rest of the year transporting cargo of all kinds across the potentially dangerous seas of Lake Michigan or the other Great Lakes. Then, come November, he would make his way to the upper Peninsula of Michigan and load the *Rouse Simmons* with trees, fitting them into every spot that could possibly contain a tree for the long trek back to Chicago. There, the docks would be full and he would be greeted by his equally gruff-but-soft-hearted friend named Claud Winters.

Schunemann and Winters

Winters was a large bearded man who had lost his leg as a child when a boxcar had run over it. He had replaced his leg with a wooden peg and this had prevented him from becoming the seafarer he had always dreamed of being. So, he had bonded with the captains such as Schunemann. And Schunemann was glad to see him every Christmas at the docks.

During other times—when it wasn't a holiday—Schunemann was known for his gruffness and for his stinginess. He was known for being stubborn and for being rough toward anyone he thought might cut in on his profits.

Schunemann was also legendary for piloting the *Rouse Simmons* through a horrid storm in 1889, making his ship the only one that was not severely damaged in that storm.

The two men had bonded over the years. In fact, it was well known that, at one time, Schunemann had given Winters a silver dollar and then told him to always keep that dollar so he would never be broke. That silver dollar had become a symbol of their friendship and when Schunemann rode into the docks, Winters would meet him and hold up the coin to show the captain that he was still not broke.

Christmas Tree Heaven

Schunemann had eventually decided to expand his empire and make the entire Christmas tree delivery a little easier. So, he had bought a plot of land in the Upper Peninsula and called it the Norther Michigan Nursery. Then, he had cut his costs even more by hiring his ship crew to head into the nursery and cut down the trees. Then, to cut costs even more, while boosting his own profits, he had begun selling the trees himself right at the dock once they were off-loaded from the *Rouse Simmons*. Schunemann's entire life had begun to revolve around the Christmas tree delivery and his entire income would double or triple with the sale of the trees during the month of November.

The year 1912 was shaping up to be a profitable one for the captain. Early snows has completely buried the tree farms in Wisconsin and Michigan. Before too long, the only trees that were looking viable and, therefore, profitable, were the ones the captain was growing at his own nursery. As November dawned, the captain was in a remarkably good mood and very optimistic about the trip north, despite the routinely poor weather and the potential danger.

So the captain had set sail for Michigan despite the constant threat of worsening weather. When he arrived at Thompson Harbor in Michigan, he found a huge crop of Christmas trees and he sent his crew into the nursery to start cutting. They had plenty to choose from and before too long the *Rouse Simmons* was being crammed with Christmas trees. The captain was so happy about the crop of trees and excited about the chance of making more money than he had in a few years that he ordered every available space of the ship's hold to be filled with trees. Then he piled the trees on the deck of the ship until the *Rouse Simmons* was lying very low in the water.

Timing was everything. With the trees cut, the captain had only a limited time to make it back to Chicago to sell the trees for the Christmas season. So, even though there were storms brewing, Schunemann ordered the ship to set sail at noon on November 22, 1912. The sky was gray; the wind was cold and strong. Snowstorms were reported all over the lake. Ice was forming on the ship even before it had left the dock as the temperature dropped and the storms worsened. Despite all of this, Schunemann was insistent in moving forward and his crew was more likely to agree with him than worry about their own safety. So the ship set sail.

Teeth of the Storm

Almost immediately the ship was in trouble. It was so weighted down by its cargo that it was unable to ride the increasingly difficult waves easily. As the water washed over the decks and the temperatures continued to drop, ice began to form across the deck, adding weight and causing the ship to ride even lower. The hatch covers on the top of the deck were not able to close properly and water began running into the hold, thus increasing the ship's weight and making it run even lower in the water. Things were looking grim very fast.

The Great Lakes are very deceptive and for those who have sailed on oceans, often underestimated. Yes, the Atlantic and Pacific are known for their unpredictable weather and strange phenomenon, but there are many tales of hardened sailors finding themselves in heaps of trouble while trying to traverse Lake Michigan or Lake Superior. Entire tankers, 700 to 800 feet long, have been known to vanish in seconds during storms on Lake Superior. Freak storms have been known to appear in the middle of Lake Michigan and take out entire fleets of pleasure-boats. When winter comes, the storms become known as gales and they are often accompanied by heavy snows and ice that help drag ships to the bottom. Even in today's modern world, with the radar and the weather satellites available, the lakes are unpredictable. They still bring about disaster.

During the time of the *Rouse Simmons,* they had no such amenities and weather prediction was more guessing and old wives tales than actual science. As the *Rouse Simmons* left docks in Michigan, they had no idea of the teeth of the storm they were sailing into. As it raised its sails, the captain was probably happy that the wind was up and he could make good time.

In Sturgeon Bay, Wisconsin, there was a tower that looked out over the lake, watching for ships flying distress flags. From there they could also dispatch rescue boats and try to save the lives of the men sailing the waters of the treacherous lakes. The night the *Rouse Simmons* attempted to bring its load of Christmas trees to Chicago, the men peering out into the terrible storm saw the ship flying a distress signal and sailing very low in the water. As soon as this was spotted, the rescue crews were dispatched. As those men tried to make their way to the struggling vessel, the waves and the storm grew worse. They soon lost sight of the *Rouse Simmons* in the blinding snow and pounding waves. They searched for two hours and came up empty.

Just as all hope seemed lost, there was a slight pause in the storm. It was like a tease from the universe. The men in the rescue boats could see the ship. According to those attempting the rescue, the boat was barely afloat and resembled a piece of floating ice. As the men attempted to shift their course and head toward the ailing vessel, the storm clamped down again as if alive. Their sight was blinded in the snow and the waves and the ship was lost from sight—this time for good.

As for life on the *Rouse Simmons,* the last few moments for the ship and crew were a misery. As the crew clung to whatever they could inside and on the ship's deck, the vessel itself rolled helplessly in the increasing waves. At some point, two sailors were sent out onto the deck and into the terrible freezing waves to check the ropes that held the Christmas trees to the deck. They were washed overboard along with most of the trees on the top deck. Once the weight was gone, the captain and crew was able to steer the ship easier and they tried to seek shelter at Bailey's Harbor. No sooner had they swung around, the wind shifted as if trying to sink the ship. The snow increased and the temperature continued to drop.

The waves began to literally pound the ship to death. As more and more of the waves washed over the deck, it left thicker and thicker sheets of ice to weigh down the ship. The top deck slowly sank lower and lower toward the roiling sea. Those on the ship must have known what was going to happen. They could see that hatch covers were not holding back the water as it battered the deck again and again. As the water flowed into the hold, it began to freeze on the trees.

Eventually, a bottle would be found, long after the ship was declared sunk and in that was a note by Captain Schunemann which read,

"Friday...everybody, good-bye. I guess we are all through. During the night the small boat was washed overboard. Leaking bad. Ingvald and Steve lost, too. God help us. Herman Schunemann."

Waiting Game

When the morning came and the ship was out of sight, everyone who had been able to see the ship before it vanished assumed the worst. Those in Chicago, however, had no idea. Claud Winters, for example, had staggered his way down to the docks to meet his friend. He had brought men with him to help the captain unload the Christmas trees and set them up around the dock to sell. The air was cold and snow was likely as Winters stood there, staring out into the cold gray waters of the lake. The men he had hired also milled around, trying to stay warm and hoping to earn a day's pay. Eventually, as the sun started to go down and the horizon still showed no *Rouse Simmons,* the men left, but Winter stayed. Winters would continue to believe that his friend and the ship would arrive even as November lead into December and Christmas approached. He continued to believe that Schunemann would find a way to survive even as debris; and then the bottle with the horrible note was found.

Barbara Schunemann, the captain's wife, was also distraught. She and her daughters became worried when the ship did not arrive. However, in those days, it was a common thing for schooners like the *Rouse Simmons* to hole up for days in various harbors while storms battered at them. They remained hopeful for a few days but then their hopes were dashed, as the remnant of Christmas trees and sodden debris began to wash up on shorelines.

As for what actually sank the ship, there are only theories. The common belief is that the ship just became too heavy with ice on the decks and frozen trees. When the wreckage was eventually found, decades later, it was laying in such a way that experts believe the water that made its way into the cargo hold and then froze and it did so mostly toward the front of the ship. The ship eventually went down nose first, sinking rapidly, and drove into the bottom of the lake.

Claud Winters spent every day through Christmas down at the docks. He was convinced that his friend would ultimately show up and expected that the masts of the schooner would appear over the horizon. He was there just after Christmas, sitting on a chair, facing the lake, when he froze to death, the silver dollar given to him by his friend clutched in his fingers. He was found the next morning and carted off, the coin falling to the ground— another level of tragedy to the sinking of the ship.

Barbara, the captain's wife, and her daughters kept up the family Christmas tree business. It appears that they used schooners a few more years, but the days of using schooners to transport Christmas trees was just about over. Chicago had undergone a Christmas tree shortage that year and transporting the trees via rail was the safer and more consistent method of transport. Barbara and her daughters in the end moved to that form of transport, bringing the trees to the spot on the docks and the family continued to sell them for many years, even after Barbara died.

These days, the legend of the *Rouse Simmons* lives on among those who still sail the lake. The schooners are long gone and the harbors in and around Chicago no longer have schooners and cargo ships. However, legends abound of ghostly ships resembling the *Rouse Simmons*, but of course, those are just legends.

What is true is that one very cold November, Santa Claus attempted to bring his cargo to Chicago for Christmas. Instead, the ship carrying those trees went down in a fierce storm and into Chicago legend.

Chapter Eight

The Eastland

In the year 1915, most of the world was on the brink of war. Although it would take an assassination for things to spill over into bloodshed, the countries of Europe had been edging their way toward conflict for a while. Each country was in the middle of an arms race which were signified most dramatically in the creation of gigantic battleships known as "dreadnoughts." In Chicago, however, this was not on the minds of the employees of Western Electric on July 24, 1915. They were worried about their company picnic which was to involve a ride in the lake to Michigan City in Indiana.

Several things happened to conspire against the ship that was hired to take the employees to Michigan City—the *S.S. Eastland*. It was a ship with a long history in the lake, and despite some complaints in the past that it was a top-heavy ship, it was considered reliable and safe. What no one entering that ship that day knew was that another famous disaster, just a few years prior, actually contributed to the tragedy that was about to occur that day.

In 1912, the *Titanic* had gone down in the icy water of the North Atlantic, taking nearly 2,000 people with it. The ship was considered "unsinkable" and, as such, it was not outfitted with enough lifeboats to rescue everyone. Thousands froze to death in the waters, their bodies left floating there. The outrage at that had caused a furor in the public and sweeping changes were made globally to ships on the oceans and lakes. Now it was required that ships carry enough lifeboats for every passenger.

The *S.S. Eastland* was commissioned shortly after the turn of the new century and was designed to be a passenger cruiser to ply the Great Lakes as a touring vessel. Throughout the early history of the ship, however, there were, as mentioned, repeated reports of the ship being top-heavy. Several crew members reported in those early days that the ship had a tendency to list to one side or another.

Lifeboats and Top-Heavy

With the *Titanic* disaster now leading to requirements for more lifeboats, the *Eastland* found itself with a problem. This meant the *S.S. Eastland* needed more lifeboats. Lacking space anywhere else for the addition of these boats, and the extra weight that came with them, they were added to the top of the boat. Thus a boat that was already top-heavy was made more so, due to the changing regulations thanks to the *Titanic* disaster.

The *S.S. Eastland* was used for parties and as a chartered cruiser. On the morning of July 24, 1915, the boat was prepared to welcome the Western Electric employees on their day-trip to Michigan City Indiana for their company picnic. Over 7,000 tickets to this event had been purchased by employees and their family members. The *S.S. Eastland* was to be one of five ships the company had chartered to take all of their employees to the spot in Indiana.

That day began very early for the crew of the *Eastland*. At three in the morning, the ship was fired up and headed toward the Chicago River and to the wharf located at Chicago and South Haven. Shortly after six in the morning, the ballast tanks within the ship were emptied. By six-thirty, nearly 5,000 people had already showed up to board the ships. The captain of the *Eastland*, wanting to keep the crowd controlled, ordered his ship to be opened up to passengers, and nearly 2,000 of those 5,000 people began to surge onto the boat.

As the passengers streamed across the walkway onto the ship, the *Eastland* began to list almost immediately to the starboard (right) side. It was listing enough that crew members and the captain were slightly concerned. The Chief Engineer, Joseph Erickson, noted the list and then ordered the crew to stabilize the ship. The crew responded immediately by filling the ballast tanks on the port (left) side. The *Eastland's* ballast tanks were relatively slow and it took three minutes before the ship began to right itself. The excursion was supposed to begin its trip to Michigan City by seven-thirty. It was now nearly seven in the morning and the ship managed to right itself for a few moments.

What happened next has been open to debate for nearly 100 years. As the thousands of passengers filtered in, they were first concentrated on the wharf side, which would be starboard, explaining why the ship first lists to that side. As the passengers entered the ship, they decided they wanted to watch other ships passing in the river or perhaps view anything but the wharf, so they began to walk toward the port side of the ship. There were some who saw a fast and fancy ship and so they suddenly surged toward the port side to look. Regardless of why the passengers (who were boarding at the rate of fifty a minute), swarmed to the port side of the ship all at once, the ship began to list dramatically to the port side. Erickson then ordered the crew to correct this list and the crew filled the other ballast tanks. Once again the ship rights itself.

Just before seven o'clock, the *Eastland* requested a tug boat to guide the ship out of the river and into Lake Michigan. At seven o'clock, the tug boat named *Kenosha* arrived and took a position at the front of the *Eastland*. No sooner did the tug boat arrive than the *Eastland* began to list to the port side again. Even though the *Eastland* was not supposed to leave the wharf until seven-thirty, Erickson ordered the engines started just after seven. Erickson then attempted, again, to correct the list to the port side. He ordered the number 3 port ballast tank to be pumped out. For some reason, the number 2 port ballast tank was not emptied.

The *Eastland* was now listing noticeably to those on shore. The Harbormaster, Adam F. Weckler, reached the Clark Street Bridge to see what was happening with the boats and their loading. He made a note of the listing of the *Eastland* and estimated the list at about seven degrees. Around this time, the total capacity of the *Eastland*, around 2,500 passengers, was reached and the crew stopped boarding. The remaining passengers are told to start boarding some of the other ships that have been chartered. Those ships were also now boarding.

It was still just about a quarter past seven. The crew was starting to worry about the list to the port side, which had become more and more pronounced with each passing minute. As the gangplanks were prepared to be brought on board, the radio operator for the *Eastland*, a man named Charles Dibbell, began to address the crowd of people huddled around the port side. He told them that they need to start moving toward the starboard side. Whether or not anyone listened or anyone followed his orders is open to debate but witnesses say that no one bothered to move and the crowd remained against the railings on the river-side of the boat.

The list of the ship was becoming more of a concern for those still on the docks. At around seven-fifteen, an employee of a business with a view of the wharf noticed the *Eastland* listing. He called over a co-worker to come look at the scene. Witnesses now estimated that the *Eastland* was listing ten to fifteen degrees to the port side.

On the *Eastland*, Erickson became alarmed enough to order the number 2 and 3 ballast tanks on the starboard side to be filled.

This time it took nearly seven minutes before water entered either of these tanks. The reason for the delay was never determined.

Just before seven-twenty, the *Eastland* does manage to right itself. Despite being straightened, the crew and captain noted that the ship felt unbalanced and unstable. Still the gangplanks were now withdrawn. The ship's captain indicated his wishes to push away from the wharf. The tug boat began to maneuver. The lines were cast off. The passengers actually made a move back to the starboard side to witness the events of the ship casting off, but the *Eastland* now began to list noticeably to the port side again.

At seven-twenty, the list to port was so pronounced that water began to wash over the main deck, through an opening placed on the deck to allow water there to wash back into the lake, known as a scupper. Chief Engineer Erickson ordered the engines stopped. Beer bottles began to crash down and the main deck was suddenly awash with water and broken glass. The remaining passengers who were still facing the port side began to move way and toward the starboard side. For some reason the ship continued to list to port, however.

The captain, a man named Pedersen, was still attempting to make way for the trip. The ship meanwhile was slowly tilting over into the water. Erickson began to issue orders that someone should herd the passengers on the forward deck toward the starboard side. Passengers near the engine room were also asked to move toward the starboard side. Meanwhile, the ship was now listing so far toward port that water was reported rushing through port gangways, and crew in the engine room reported water was entering the room from the port side. A crew member opened an alarm whistle known as a Modoc Whistle to warn anyone within earshot that something was horribly wrong with the *Eastland*.

A Party Till the End

Captain Pedersen was still trying to move forward with the excursion. It was now just before seven-thirty and Pedersen ordered the engine room to stand by for further orders. He ordered any remaining lines cast off. Pedersen also called for the opening of the Clark Street Bridge so the ship could pass beneath. This order was refused by the harbormaster, however, because of the obvious and pronounced list of the ship. Witnesses on shore would later state that, by that point, the ship's list was twenty-five to thirty degrees to port. The

Eastland's stern, the side where all lines had already been cast off, began to move out into the river. The passengers, believing the ship to be moving out into the river to leave made another surge toward port.

At seven twenty-five the ship made its last attempt to correct the list. Once again the list was corrected, but for only a few moments. The ship began to list to port again almost immediately. More water came rushing into the ship through gangways. Erickson ordered a pump to be activated to attempt to pump out the water. The ship was moving very quickly now, and after this last attempt to correct itself, the ship was almost immediately again at a twenty-five to thirty-degree list to port. The crew members in the boiler room were barely able to stand. Sensing that the ship was lost due to the water rushing into the engine room and the severe list, the stokers and oilers began to rush up to the main deck.

Once again the passengers were asked to move to the starboard side. Several passengers attempt to comply but the decks were slick with water and the list was too severe. Those on the decks were unable to negotiate the incline and move. The ship's orchestra started to play music but the musicians were having a difficult time standing. There was not yet a panic among the passengers but many in and around the area sensed that something was horribly wrong.

At seven-twenty-eight on that morning, the angle of the ship reached forty-five degrees. Everything within the ship that was not nailed down began to crash to the floor. The dishes in the kitchen fell out of the racks. The piano on the promenade deck went sliding across the deck and nearly crushed two women. The refrigerator behind the ship's bar turned over with a huge crash. This was the first real alert to the passengers that the ship is doomed. Now panic ensued. Water was now pouring in uncontrolled in the gangways and portholes. Passengers made a frantic effort to get starboard. The passengers on the main deck rushed to the staircases that lead to the 'tween deck.

Past the Point of No Return

Things happened rapidly now. The *Eastland* was past the point of saving. The captain screamed toward the wharf that gangways be brought back to the ship. The ship was tilting too rapidly for anyone to do anything. Crew members and passengers began to jump off the ship into the river. The passengers and crew were also jumping off on the starboard side of the ship. As this happened, water continued to rush in on the port side and the passengers left there added to the weight.

It was now seven-thirty and the *Eastland* rolled slowly and quietly onto its port side. The ship rested in the muddy Chicago River bottom. The ship was in just twenty feet of water and is only 19.2 feet from the wharf. The tug boat casts off its lines and heads to the wharf. This allowed some passengers still on the ship to use the tug boat as a kind of bridge to the wharf.

The *Eastland* turned on it side so quickly that no lifeboats were launched and no life-vests were handed out. The river was immediately flooded with passengers. However, the wake of the capsizing ship created a lot of waves. Most of the passengers were dressed in their "Sunday" finest for the day, which, in that day, meant heavy suits and dresses. Waves swamp many in the river. Others are sucked out in the current and pulled under. Inside the ship those who moved to the staircases were hopelessly trapped as the water rushed in. The greatest concentration of dead were found in these locations.

Inside the ship, men, women, and children were heard screaming. The water was rushing in. The passengers were piled in entrance-ways and exits. As helpless bystanders attempted to climb onto the side of the ship, they could hear the passengers inside screaming. Slowly, dreadfully, the screaming began to stop as those inside are pulled into the water that has filled the ship and drown.

Firemen began to arrive. A police diver was called. Workers from nearby construction sites were called and brought torches to start cutting holes in the starboard side of the ship which is still sticking out of the water. They moved frantically and tried to pull passengers out. The work was slow. While some passengers were pulled out of the holes it became evident that this was no longer a rescue mission, but a recovery mission.

Other ships were called and began to pluck passengers floating in the river. Some were rescued, but many were hopelessly swept under thanks to the river's strong current. The river was dragged using large grappling hooks. Rescuers from the shore were diving into the river and climbing onto the side of the ship where they began the terrible task of pulling bodies out of the hull.

A Tragedy Reviewed

The next few days were filled with tragedy and horror. In the disaster, 844 passengers were drowned, and 22 entire families were wiped out.

Rumors abound of the horrors faced by those trying to recover bodies of pulling men, women and many, many children out of the hull. One legend has it that the police diver who was brought in to help with the recovery, after spending a day pulling out bodies, broke down in hysterics and was driven mad. Reportedly, he was sedated and hospitalized.

In the months that followed, the Captain does not do well for himself by blaming the passengers rather than taking any blame for the disaster himself. Since many of the passengers were immigrants, he blamed their ignorance and "questionable" character for the disaster rather than the fact he was still trying to cast off while the ship was lost. The blame for this disaster was never truly affixed to one thing, but spread around among several areas.

The ship was called top-heavy. The ship's ballast system is declared inadequate. Modifications done to the *Eastland* to make the ship faster added more weight to the top of the ship and that is blamed for increasing the top-heaviness of the ship.

Regardless of the reasons, the day of July 24th was one of the worst disasters in shipping history within the United States. The fact that it took place less than twenty feet from shore is a strange and cruel irony. There were so many bodies that it took days and weeks to identify them. Warehouses now used by Oprah's Harpo Studios were used to store bodies because there was no room at the morgues.

Eventually, the *Eastland* was righted and repaired. The name of the ship was changed to the *Wilmette* and it was used as a gunboat and pressed back into service. Ultimately, the ship was decommissioned and turned into scrap.

The story of the *Eastland* passed into history. However, due to the passengers being immigrants, whereas many passengers on the *Titanic* were rich, the story was not given as much coverage nationally. Of course, events in other parts of the world were also taking up the minds of most as World War One raged in Europe.

Today one of the largest collections of *Eastland*-related material can be found at the Chicago Historical Society. The Chicago Maritime Society also has a very large collection of artifacts from the *Eastland* disaster. Both of these organizations can be visited and found online.

Chapter Nine

The Fresh Water Tidal Wave

Lake Michigan, as has been stated, is essentially a large inland sea. The term "lake" tends to make people think that it's safe and that nothing dangerous can happen. They forget just how large the lake is and how deep. They don't know about the strange weather than can happen in the middle of the body of water. They don't know about the freak storms or the lake's penchant for swallowing ships whole and not letting so much as a lifeboat to the surface. Certainly, the last thing they think of is anything resembling a tidal wave.

Then again, the general public probably doesn't know what a real tidal wave looks like. They think of the giant monster waves likely to send cruise ships upside down so that surviving passenger can crawl their way to toward the propeller area to be rescued. If they were paying attention to the world just a few years ago and saw the tidal wave that hit such a huge portion of Asia, then they might know that giant waves need not be associated with tidal wave. They need only be huge sheets of water moving inexorably onto shore with incredible power, sweeping away men and women and anything else in their paths.

A tidal wave is the sudden receding of water from areas such as beaches. The phenomenon is known to increase the death toll because people come down to the beach to see the water receding. Then, suddenly, the hold that causes the water to recede lets go and the water come rushing back, with incredible speed and power. In the ocean, these are caused by earthquakes under the sea or perhaps large shelves of ice falling into the ocean near places like the Arctic or Antarctic.

In places like Chicago, there are very few earthquakes. Yes, there are fault lines beneath even the Midwest, but they are not nearly as deep as beneath the ocean waves. So, while tidal waves in the strictest sense are unlikely on Lake Michigan, there is something very similar and, potentially, just as deadly that can occur. Just such a thing did occur one fine Saturday morning in June of 1954.

The Midwest is known for very strong, powerful storms that form throughout the year. These storms develop quickly, form powerful lines, move through the cities and towns quickly, leaving destruction behind them, and then vanish just as quickly. When they happen during the spring and summer, they bring strong thunderstorms. When these quick-moving storms come through in the winter, they often leave cities like Chicago buried in snow.

When these storms come roaring through Chicago, the winds they push before them create intense barometric pressure. This pressure pushes down on the buildings and people, but most don't even feel it. When it becomes a problem is when the storm hits the lake. The downward pressure acts much like the earthquake does with a tsunami in the ocean. It begins to push the water away from the Chicago shores and all of the various beaches on the westerly edge of the lake. The water builds and builds and pushes more and more water ahead of it. When the storm finally reaches the other side of the lake, or dissipates over the water, all of that water that had been pushing forward suddenly rushes back to where it was before. In essence, what you have is a wall of water covering huge distances in seconds just like a tsunami. However, when they happen on a lake, they are known as seiches.

These days seiches are predictable. When the fast-moving storms come through, the warnings are often issues for towns and cities all along the lake. However, back in 1954, predicting the weather was still a theory more than it was a science. A seiche was considered so rare and so unlikely that it was not generally considered a danger.

The 1954 Storm

The wave hit the shoreline that morning at about 9:30 a.m. That morning had been a stormy one. A squall line had moved through the area moving from the northeast to the southwest. It was powerful enough to generate sixty mile-per-hour winds and began pushing water ahead of it in a wave about six-feet high toward Michigan City, Indiana. That wall of water hit the beaches there about 8:10. The storms moved on shore then and the water reacted like a rubber band that had been stretched too far. It snapped back once the pressure was gone and began rocketing back toward Chicago.

In Chicago at that time, it was not unheard of for those interested in fishing to show up early in the morning and line the various piers and harbors that stretch out into the lake. That morning there was a particularly nice crowd of anglers gathered at the pier known as North Avenue Beach. Fathers and sons stood there in the passing of the storm and fished happily in the lake. They had no idea that a wall of water now reaching almost ten feet was headed right for them like something alive and hungry.

The difference between a tsunami and a seiche, besides how they are formed, is the speed at which they travel. Tsunamis travel like bullet trains found in Asia and come on shore at speeds more likely to be found on racetracks than in lakes. Seiches travel quickly, but much more slowly than that. It took a full eighty minutes for the water that had been pushed to Michigan City to come back to Chicago's shores. The distance between Chicago and Michigan City is roughly forty miles which means that the wave was traveling about thirty-miles-per-hour.

The lake began to get choppy as the wave made its way back toward those fishing and enjoying the day beside the lake. According to those who witnessed the event a huge wave was not coming to crash on shore. The fishermen were lined up along a pier that extended out into the lake, surrounded on almost all sides by water. As they stood there, the water suddenly rose, taking with it piers, boats and, of course, fishermen.

According to witnesses who were pulling up to the harbor, the scene was chaos and confusion. Some said that the area just beyond the parking lot was filled with water. There were people running everywhere. Still others were running away from the water, while more were running toward the area. Out in the lake, the yachts and boats were bobbing wildly against their moorings or in the lake itself. The air was filled with people screaming.

Several fishermen had been lying on their stomachs as they tried to guide their lines to where they felt the fish might be. Suddenly the water had simply risen with amazing speed and washed over them. The best guess was that twenty fishermen were washed into the lake.

Area rescue teams were called. Helicopters were put into the air and boats were cast off to find the fishermen who were missing. However, the wave was so powerful and the men had been washed so far away, they were very hard to find. Twelve of those who were fishing one moment and then in the lake the next were pulled out of the water. The remaining eight were killed, drowned in the monster wave that had ruined the beautiful morning.

Seiches—Rare But Deadly

Seiches of the kind which hit that day are very rare. Even when they do happen, having them be so severe that they cause a loss of life is even more rare. There have been improvements, of course, in weather forecasting since that fateful day. As such, the seiches are often predicted well in advance which allows for greater warnings and caution. Since a seiche is caused by an atmospheric disturbance, the lake shore actually gets hundreds of them every year, but they seldom are more than a few feet and most people probably don't even notice them.

Weather in the Midwest is often strange and it can, at times, be deadly. Sudden storms are known and well documented in the middle of the Great Lakes. However, very few events as odd as the one that swept eight men to their deaths have happened even in the Midwest. In some ways, it just proves that life moves quickly, and the end can come even when the day seems pleasant and you just want to do a little fishing.

Chapter Ten

The Blizzard

In the Midwest, water comes in many forms. There are storms that drop rain and cause floods. There are rivers that can overflow. There are lakes which form seiches and can flood sub-basements. The Midwest, however, also has something not seen in some parts of the country: seasons. This includes winter and water falls during that time of year as well.

The problem is that when this water falls, it solidifies in the cold arctic air that comes rushing down out of Canada and the Arctic Circle. That moisture becomes ice, freezing rain and, most often, snow. Chicago is notorious for its harsh winters and that reputation has been earned even if it isn't actually true every year.

While nearly every winter the city gets some heavy snowfalls, there are times when bigger storms than normal come through. When they do, they sometime shut down the entire city and cause people to stay indoors. They happen every so often, but they normally last for a few days and they are generally few and far between.

The problem with the snow and winter weather in Chicago is that it is accompanied by paralyzing cold. This makes cleaning up the snow difficult. It also prevents the snow from melting, so that when snows come later, they often just pile up on the snow already on the ground.

In January of 1918, a blizzard hit and dumped 42 inches of snow. As the 1970s ended, a series of snows and one significant snow during January of 1979 buried the city under 20.3 inches. Before the winter was over, in 1979, there was a total of 29 inches on the ground. These were all very bad and caused problems for a lot of people. However, nothing has ever compared with what happened in 1967.

Storm of 1967

In January 1967, a storm of epic proportions came across the city and set records that stand to this day. It was a Thursday, January 26th, and the weather forecast certainly had nothing to say that would have caused anyone in the city of Chicago any concern. The forecast said the snow would be fairly light with the possibility of four inches when the storm was over. The snow started early, at 5:02 a.m that Thursday.

It had been a strange winter so far. Just a few days before the snow fell, the air temperature had reached into the sixties. Then there had been a series of thunderstorms. In parts south of the city, tornado warnings had been issued. Now the temperature had plummeted and winter had returned with a vengeance.

Very likely, the citizens of Chicago crawled out of bed, looked out their windows, groaned at the snow, and then set about trying to get to work. This was winter in Chicago. Chicagoans take a certain pride in surviving the snow. They laugh at the other cities that seem paralyzed by even just a few inches. So, the city set about their daily activities. What they did not know, however, was that this storm was unlike anything the city had seen before.

These days the weathermen have Doppler radar and other ways to develop an accurate feel for a storm's intensity. In 1967, even the weather radar screens were little more than greenish blobs on screens that most couldn't accurately read. There was little to tell those trying to forecast the weather that this was a once-in-a-lifetime event.

As the day wore on, it soon became evident that something was different. The snow was falling faster and harder than anyone had seen before. Before too long, traffic became a snarl that was unbearable. As drivers of cars, trucks, and buses sat still in traffic, the snow began to pile up against their cars. Before too long, the cars and trucks and buses couldn't even move. Drivers began abandoning their vehicles where they were sitting and left them in the middle of the road. At first the snow made it difficult to drive, and then roads became impassable because they were criss-crossed with vehicles that were now becoming buried in snow.

Those who had to, made it to work and thought that the storm might die down to let them get back home. But they looked out their windows at streets clogged with abandoned cars and ever-increasing drifts of snow, and decided it might be best to stay at the office. Some thought it might just be working late. Then the snow kept coming and coming and coming. The snow did not stop until Friday morning.

Schools found themselves filled with students who could not make it home. The buses couldn't run and their parents couldn't make the trips to the school to pick them up. Some school districts began setting up shelters, cots, and sleeping bags in gymnasiums. In south suburban Markham, for example, 650 students scattered about in four schools stayed in the library and gym. The schools did their best to make the students comfortable and keep them entertained.

Some places throughout the city were not faring as well. Looters were spotted as the streets became abandoned. At grocery stores people began thronging into the stores to buy up the last of the supplies they felt they might need to stay indoors. The stores soon found themselves with no food and empty shelves. Even more tragically, twenty-six people lost their lives. Some died from heart attacks while shoveling snow. A ten-year-old girl died when police and looters exchanged gunfire. A minister was run down by a snowplow who didn't see him beneath the snow. Others also froze while trying to trudge their way through the snow.

The third largest city in the country was completely shut down. Both airports were immobile. The airports set up areas for travelers to sleep in the airport and did their best to provide services for them so that they could be as comfortable as possible. Hotels and motels in and around the airports were jammed with stranded travelers. Reportedly, at Midway Airport, snow drifts as high as ten feet covered the runways.

Downtown Chicago was like something out of a movie. Cars, barely visible in drifts burying them to their rooftops, littered the middle of the streets. The sidewalks and streets were empty for days. Everyone who worked downtown had managed to get home before too long. The city was empty and covered in white.

Snowplows found it nearly impossible to plow. Since row upon row of cars littered the highways and streets and side-streets, they were unable to push down streets and clear them. People were stuck in their homes. Elderly neighbors had no way to get out, get to stores, or clear the snow from in front of their homes.

Mayor Daley did what he could. He got on television and was honest with his citizens. He told them that the city services were taxed to the maximum. Therefore, they called on the citizens to help each other. He asked them to check on neighbors. He told them to shovel each other's walkways and sidewalks. In modern times this might have been greeted with sneers and cynicism, but during this blizzard and in this city, the people responded positively. The citizens did band together and try to help each other.

Slowly but surely the city began to dig itself out. Tow trucks were called in to help pull cars and trucks to the sides of roads so the snowplows could get through. Eventually, the roads were cleared. The sidewalks soon followed. Neighbors chipped in and tried to make the best of it. The blizzard became another point in the city's history and a point of pride for those who made it through.

1979 Miserable Winter Weather

Years later, in 1979, however, things did not go so well. It was another miserable winter. Many feet of snow were already on the ground as one large snowstorm after another hit the city followed by deep freezes that prevented the snow from being cleared. Then, a huge storm hit in early January and truly buried the city.

This time, the mayor, who was not Daley, did not get on television and ask for calm. Instead, he was seen heading out of town. The city was miserable and the city did not respond as it had during the late-sixties storm. The citizens began to rebel against the mayor.

During the next election, mayoral candidate Jane Byrne, ran a campaign based almost entirely on the fact that her predecessor had left town when the city was buried in snow. She became the city's first female mayor and it became a priority for every mayor thereafter to make sure that the city services were prepared for any predicted blizzard. In Chicago, people take their snow very, very seriously. It can even cost you re-election.

Chapter Eleven

The Great Chicago Flood

It was a Monday, April 13, 1992, and things were moving along as usual in downtown Chicago. The downtown area, known as the Loop, was bustling with people going to work. The roads were crowded. People moved from office building to office building. They were preparing to start another week. What they didn't know was that they were about to experience one of the costliest disasters in Chicago history. No one would die, but the ultimate cost of this disaster would end up in the range of one billion dollars.

The idea was to remove some of the old pilings in the Chicago River very closely to the downtown buildings. This is the same general area where the *Eastland* had gone down. Arrangements were made to put new pilings for cruise ships and other boats that were being used to ferry tourists around and into the lake. So, contractors were hired to head out into the waterway and remove the pilings. It seemed like a simple thing and a simple solution, but it was about to shut down the entire city.

Much of the city did not know that downtown Chicago lay over a network of tunnels. As most people probably know, the city does not have a huge network of underground subway tunnels. Most of the trains are elevated, running above the street and, thus, Chicago's famous "EL." But that didn't mean that there weren't other rail systems hidden below the Chicago streets in the area known as the Loop.

The tunnels were used to transport things like mail and packages, messages, and other materials between the various office buildings and shopping centers that comprised downtown Chicago. Over the years, other things had come into place that replaced the need for the underground tunnel system. As such, much of them had been abandoned and forgotten. So, on that day when the contractors were about to make the most expensive mistake in the history of the city, very few knew that a network of tunnels connected nearly all of the basements in downtown Chicago to the Chicago River.

The contractors were working on a barge floating in the river. They were removing the concrete pilings. None of them were aware of the tunnels and the old, worn down, fragile wall that blocked the tunnels from the river. One of the pilings, along the east bank, was right next to that wall and the wall itself was starting to crumble and wear down. When the piling was removed, it did not hit the wall directly, but the pressure wave caused in the water made the crumbling structure crack. Water began spraying into the tunnel. Not only water, but mud from the bottom of the river and from the water that had been churned up from the piling removal.

Oozing Mud, Then Water

The water actually leaked into the tunnel very slowly at first. In fact, the area had probably been leaking for weeks before the disaster itself shut down the city. This was likely due to the soft mud gradually oozing through the crack slowing the water. By April 13th, however, all of the mud had managed to creep its way inside the tunnel. Now there was nothing to hold back the river.

Before the water started flowing and while mud was still oozing through the hole, a telecommunications employee actually spotted the leak. He brought a videotape camera with him and taped the image of the mud and water slowly making its way into the tunnel. He sent the tape to officials at the city. However, those officials looked at the tape and determined the leak was not serious and nothing to be worried about. In fact, they started a bidding process to find someone to repair the tunnel, which is a process that can take months to complete. Those tunnels were not well documented and some of them were even built illegally and violated rules of private property.

On April 13th, the water finally found a way in. The Chicago River began pouring into the tunnels and then rushed through the corridors into the basements of Loop office buildings and stores. There was also an underground shopping area with walkways that connected the many offices and buildings and this began to flood as well. The Chicago financial district was at risk and there was fear that the water could cause an electrical shortage. The basements were soon flooded to the top with muddy, dirty river water. Exactly how far-reaching the tunnels were, no one knew, but they would soon find out.

Evacuations

The water moved rapidly through the tunnels and it was soon noticed. The city acted quickly and began evacuating the city. There were fears that electrical shortages would have shut down entire buildings, trapping people in elevators, or causing electrocutions. The financial district was evacuated first and the city moved to get people out of the downtown area so they could shut down electricity and natural gas.

The trading stopped at the Chicago Board of Trade and the Mercantile Exchange. Soon buildings around downtown were reporting nearly forty feet of water in their lower levels and sub-basements. All of this was happening below ground and to those who were working and walking the streets, nothing seemed to be wrong.

At first, no one knew where the water was coming from. When workers managed to make their way down into the tunnels they found fish amidst the mud and dirt. Soon it was obvious this was not a broken water pipe or anything of that nature. They soon traced the leak back to the river. Once they realized what was happening, another dangerous situation was spotted.

While most of the public transportation trains in downtown Chicago were elevated, during the 1940s some underground lines had been built and many of the tunnels were walled off. However, these concrete blocks to the tunnels had not been maintained as regularly as other areas. Soon, a crack was found in one of those walls and water began pouring into one of the CTA subway tunnels. It would not be long before commuters found themselves stranded and trying to find alternate ways home as the system was shut down.

Bewildered workers began filling the streets, being told they needed to evacuate. The public was confused at first, but then something interesting happened. WMAQ reporter Larry Langford, normally a crime reporter working overnight, had been listening to his fire and police scanners when he started to hear about office buildings being evacuated and he headed downtown.

Langford reached downtown and reported that city officials were looking for a leak and were shutting down water mains all around the city to see if that would stop the flooding. As Langford watched those city officials trying to find the leak he heard a report about Merchandise Mart employees reporting several feet of water in the basement. The first reports of fish in the water came at this point. Langford made the trek over to the Merchandise Mart to check out the reports. The Mart just happened to be near where the piling had been removed and as he stood outside the Merchandise Mart he looked down at the river and saw something strange.

A Scary Leak

He saw what looked like a whirlpool. In fact, during his report, he stated it looked like a bathtub being drained with the water turning and slowly filtering into what appeared to be a concrete wall along the river. He reported that it appeared as if the Chicago River were emptying into the tunnels and that there were reports of fish in the water in the basements. This was how the city knew, including officials, that the Chicago River was the source of the leak and that this could be much more serious than anyone first thought.

Downtown Chicago is more than just offices and stores. There are also condos and apartment buildings. The Chicago Police Department and other officials for the city began walking from building to building and evacuating people. Loudspeakers and police cars with speakers began patrolling the streets telling people that they needed to leave the buildings in an orderly fashion. Fortunately, there was no panic and no one started trouble. Instead, workers and residents simply filed into the streets and found their way home or found other places to stay.

The various building managers started to try to assist with the problem by turning on their sump pumps. Unfortunately, this was proving ineffective. Thousands upon thousands of gallons of water were pouring into the basements and sub-basements. Of course, in those sub-basements were where the engineering departments of those buildings were located and were thick with cables and wires and electronics. Most of downtown Chicago was buried in thirty to forty feet of water before that Monday afternoon had arrived. In most places the water was rising at a rate of four feet an hour. By the time it was all said and done, over 250 million gallons of water were out of the river and in the basements of office buildings and stores throughout the area. Stores like Marshall Field's and Carsons—staples of downtown Chicago's shopping district—were shut down as their basements were completely submerged.

The rest of the entire city was soon in danger of being shut down. City Hall was also located in the flood zone. The Art Institute of Chicago was shut down. The Board of Trade had been closed and gone dark. The Sate of Illinois Building, the center for many offices that run the entire state of Illinois, was shut down and the offices closed. The subway system throughout downtown was shut down until further notice. Effectively, the entire city, the city government, and all of the downtown area was at a standstill while engineers frantically tried to slow and then stop the flow of water into the tunnels. The pumps were not working because the water was replaced as soon as it was pumped out.

Stopping the Flow

Workers showed up on a barge near where the barge had been that ripped the piling out in the first place. They began trying to stop the flow of the water. Sixty-five truckloads of rocks and cement arrived near the hole in the wall. They began dumping the rocks, gravel, and cement into the river, trying to place the obstacles in front of the hole in the wall. They even began throwing mattresses in the river in an attempt to wedge them into the hole that had now grown to about twenty feet wide.

The Army Corps of Engineers was contacted for assistance. They agreed to have the locks on the river to keep the Chicago River flowing toward the Mississippi (instead of into the Lake) closed. Two locks, one at Lake Michigan and then opening up the locks downstream from downtown slowed the flow of the river and, thus, the flow of the water into the hole in the wall.

For years, Chicago had been building a massive underground system to manage water overflows during storms and other emergencies known as "Deep Tunnel." It is still one of the largest construction projects in the country. Once the hole had been plugged and the flood slowed to a trickle, the pumps were brought in and the water was pumped into this second, larger tunnel system meant to expressly handle this kind of situation. This succeeded in stopping the flooding and diverting the water, but the clean-up was going to take longer than three days for the water to start to recede.

Eventually, a company called Kenny Construction stepped up and started drilling shafts into the flooded tunnels. They then started putting plugs into the tunnels and that helped stop the flooding entirely. Now the water was drained, slowly, filling the Deep Tunnel but receding from the basements and sub-basements. After the three days had gone by, the businesses in the Loop were allowed to start again, and stores were allowed to open.

The cost to the city would run into the billions and this quickly became the costliest disaster in the history of Chicago. Several offices and buildings were closed for weeks. The Art Institute of Chicago, one of the premier tourist attractions in the city, was closed "indefinitely" as it needed to take a look at the art collections that were damaged after being stored in the basement. Even some of the television stations located in the flood area were shut down and limited in their news coverage of the event. Since the incident had happened on tax day, the IRS granted natural disaster extensions to the city and those who had been affected by the disaster.

Lesson Learned

In the end, the estimate was that the disaster cost the city $1.95 billion. The city had to recognize that the underground areas of Chicago needed to be watched over more carefully. The city stepped forward and took control of the tunnels system and began doing regular maintenance. Hatches were installed at all of the areas where the tunnels touched the river to prevent flooding in the future.

Investigations were begun to try and determine who was at fault for the disaster. Yes, the construction contractors had removed the piling, but the wall itself was crumbling already. The workers also had faulty and out-dated maps provided by the city which had long ago forgotten that the tunnels were even there. To this day, no one has really been held responsible and no one was prosecuted for shutting down the third largest city in the country for three days.

Evacuation procedures were put into place to help the downtown area should any sort of disaster happen like that again. After the disasters in New York on September 11, 2001, even more procedures were put into place. There have been subsequent disasters, such as a fire in the subway system, where evacuations were handled properly and safely. The lessons learned on the day of the flood were built upon to make the city safer down the road.

In the end, the city learned that it didn't take a spectacular disaster like a plane crash or fire to bring the city to a standstill. Although no one lost their life during this disaster, the city took weeks to recover and for business to truly get back to normal. It proved to city officials that there needed to be procedures in place to keep the city going even if the disaster was happening beneath the streets. It proved that Chicago was definitely a city of water.

Part Three

City of Air

At times throughout its history, the city of Chicago has been a center for transportation. Its centralized location helped at least a bit. However, it was also close to major waterways and had canals and rivers nearby that connected to other waterways. The Chicago River could connect boats and barges to the Mississippi River fairly easily. Lake Michigan was a major center for transporting goods and people for decades. When the railroads ruled transportation in this country, it was said that all tracks eventually lead to Chicago.

When air travel became something of the norm, it seemed natural then for Chicago to follow this tradition and to become some kind of air hub. These days, of course, most people know that Midway and then O'Hare airports were major air hubs at different times in Chicago's history. Both airports are still major hubs for numerous major airlines.

Air has become a major factor in the history of Chicago. As airplanes became the norm, the city shifted from rail to planes almost naturally. At the same time, the air itself has changed portions of Chicago throughout its history.

The element of air is a strange thing. Quite simply put, we cannot survive without it. We need it to live and yet we cannot see it. We trust it to be there, but we have no idea if it is without either breathing whatever is around us or by using meters to detect oxygen. We do, however, see and feel the effects of air.

We see the storms that come through cities and towns across the country and the effect air has when it decides to turn destructive. We see how air supports airplanes and airships and we see what happens when that air decides its time for those devices to fall from the sky. We can feel the wind and we know that air, like fire and like water, can bring good and that it is essential for our life—but that it can turn deadly when it needs to.

Chicago has been affected by air. It has prospered from a human's desire to conquer air and master it and travel through it. However, it has seen the terrible effects of air as well. At times, those effects have shocked the nation, or changed entire neighborhoods and families in this great city for all time. As much as it is a city of fire and a city of water, Chicago is definitely also a city of air.

Chapter Twelve

The Airship

It is amazing to think in today's world that, at one time, airships or blimps were considered the future of air travel. Of course, we all have the benefit of hindsight to see how foolish this thought was given the desire, at least back then to use flammable and dangerous gases to keep those ships in the air. However, airplanes were seen as rickety and uncertain things that could carry only a few people safely. Planes were seen mostly as ways to carry cargo and mail across distances, but passengers were expected to float gently, as if on an ocean of air, in giant rigid dirigibles that would take them across oceans or across countries.

Some of those airships were truly impressive. The most famous, the *Hindenburg*, was a luxurious transportation device on par with some of the finest ocean liners of its day. There were state rooms with sinks and running water and comfortable beds. There were dining rooms with real china and crystal. There was an area for entertainment and live performances. There were sitting rooms and even a smoking room with an electric lighter to prevent any open flames in a ship filled with explosive hydrogen.

In 1919, the airships had yet to reach the dimensions that the Germans eventually would by the 1930s. Still, the Goodyear Tire and Rubber Company was on top of the trend from the very start. They had produced airships and blimps that were used during World War I for the U.S. Navy in spotting submarines. They also saw the immense advertising possibilities when they saw the huge crowds that would gather to watch the blimps and airships they designed and flew. On July 21, 1919, the company chose Chicago as a place to test one of its newest airship designs, the *Wingfoot Air Express*.

The Wingfoot Express

The *Wingfoot Air Express* was a new design for the Goodyear company. It was filled with hydrogen, which was common, but had a design that outfitted the blimp with something known as "ballonets" which were compartments to hold the gas. The design was meant to keep the ship in the air should any one of the compartments start to leak. Also, the airship had a new layout and design for the engines, with the propellers in front of the engines rather than behind them.

Normally, for testing purposes, the Goodyear company used a field in Akron, Ohio. However, the war had just ended a few months prior and the facility was still being used and managed by the U.S. Navy and in government hands. So, to test this new design, the company was seeking facilities with a hangar large enough to contain the blimp. They found such a place on Chicago's south side near an amusement park known as White City.

The *Wingfoot Air Express* was definitely more like a blimp than the airships many associate with the Zeppelins that would come later. It was big, but the passengers and crew rode in a gondola slung beneath the balloon. The gondola had room enough for the crew and thirteen passengers. This morning, however, the *Wingfoot* would have a very small number of passengers. The task was simple and that was to take it out of the hangar, fly it to Grant Park, inspect the ship, take off, fly around the city a bit and then head back to White City. In all, it was to have been a very uneventful trip.

It was hot that day, which is typical of life in Chicago during the summer. Many people were doing whatever they could to spend the day outside to get a bit of a cool breeze. Others had windows open to try and do the same. It was already hot by nine in the morning when the *Wingfoot Air Express* was taken from the hangar and pilot John A. Boettner put on a parachute, climbed over the railing of the gondola and took up his position at the wheel. The sun was out and, despite the heat, it looked like the perfect day to fly.

Two mechanics for Goodyear, Henry Wacker and Carl "Buck" Weaver were also putting on their chutes and they soon joined the pilot by climbing over the railing. The men had one passenger at that point and he was a colonel in the Army named Joseph Morrow. He had never ridden in an airship and he had received permission from Goodyear to fly in this one that day.

The Trip

The ship was pulled from the hangar as a crowd began to form to watch the ship take off. The riggers tugged the cables and ropes that held the *Wingfoot* earthbound. As the sun rose higher in the sky, the engines were primed and then the propellers kicked into life. The steady hum and noise of the engines soon filled the air as the crowd *oohed and ahhed*. Once Boettner checked his controls, then the wind and the weather, he decided that it was time to take off and he gave a signal to the crew holding the lines. The stern swung free and began to rise first and then, soon after, the ropes holding the bow began to rise and the *Wingfoot* rose into the air.

The *Wingfoot* looked majestic that morning as it rose into the humid air. The speed of the ship would, according to witnesses, not reach about forty-five miles per hour. The ship made a turn and headed east and then made another turn to the north as the Lake approached. The first part of the flight was to travel parallel to Michigan Avenue. They were immediately visible to the people who had made their way down near the lake to try and catch a cool breeze. Their first stop was to be Grant Park, which, at that time, was also an airfield. In fact, the plan, at one time, was to make Grant Park a regular stopping point for airships like the *Wingfoot*. For years, the field was also a place where regular airplane races were held.

The airship trundled slowly toward Grant Park. Below, the people walking the streets looked up and pointed at the ship. It began to descend slowly, the park appearing and then growing larger from the windows of the gondola. The ground crews came out, shielding their eyes against the sun and waited for the mooring ropes to descend from the ship. Once they did, they began to assist in pulling the gas-filled airship to earth.

Once the ship was grounded, and in view of another crowd, the pilot and the crew climbed back over the gondola railing and began to visually inspect the engines and the rest of the ship. Noon was approaching and the heat of the day was getting intense as the men looked over the skin of the ship and listened to the hum and noise of the engines. The colonel was allowed to disembark at that time and he did thank his pilot and crew and then stood with the crowd to see the airship ascend again.

All appeared well and just before noon finally hit, the *Wingfoot* was once again allowed to float free from its moorings and into the air. It swung north again, toward Diversey Avenue, giving more people who were walking along or near the lake, or through downtown, a great view as it glided along the lake.

Once it reached Diversey, the ship turned around, and began its run back toward Grant Park where it was scheduled to dock once again for further inspections. The ship once again descended. It was just around three in the afternoon as the crew grabbed the mooring ropes for the second time and tied the ship to the ground. Once again the ship was inspected and two more passengers were picked up to make the final flight back to White City. One was Earl Davenport, who worked as a publicity manager for Goodyear and the other was a photographer for the *Chicago Herald and Examiner*, William Norton.

The ship was once again deemed sound and the mooring ropes were let go. For the third time that day, the *Wingfoot Air Express* would ascend into the humid air and delight the crowds. Once the ship had ascended, the reporter, Norton, would make a fateful request that the pilot would grant. He wanted to get some aerial shots of the famous Chicago skyscrapers, so he asked the pilot if the ship could fly over downtown instead of hugging the lake. For whatever reason, the pilot agreed and the ship made a slight turn and began flying over the area known as the Loop, much to the delight of employees in downtown Chicago who were already starting to head home as the end of the work day approached.

The ship began to fly over the financial district. The streets were full of people finishing their business in the banks located in that area as well as workers heading home. They craned their necks up to stare into the blazing sky and see the ship as it glided gracefully over the buildings. Many looked up and pointed, letting out shouts of excitement. The various parks that littered the area at that time, providing patches of green where breezes could be found, were packed with those trying to find respite from the heat.

Whatever happened, happened very fast. Much like the Hindenburg disaster that would become famous decades later, once a flame was spotted, the ship itself was lost in mere seconds. The information told by the pilot later would differ from the witnesses on the ground. All that is known is that, somehow, and somewhere, a flame was spotted on the ship. As soon as it was seen, the ship itself was lost.

Destruction and Loss

As stunned onlookers at first gasped and then began to scream, the *Wingfoot Air Express* burst into flames, buckled, and began to plummet from the skies, directly over the buildings the photographer Norton wanted to photograph. The men inside began to fall from the gondola, plummeting and then stopping as their parachutes opened. Four men were soon falling through the skies and then descending slowly as their chutes opened. Then the horror truly began as the flaming wreckage fell to earth like a meteor, burning the chutes of those men and heading straight for one of the skyscrapers.

Inside the building holding the Illinois Trust and Savings bank, the workers were getting ready to head home. The last of the financial transactions had been completed and the doors had been closed to further customers. The ladies who worked behind the massive glass and metal cage that was in the center of the huge marble room were busy doing the last minute things they needed to do before finally heading out the door and then home after a busy day.

Above them, the massive glass and metal skylight that comprised much of the roof let in a steady stream of light that kept the immense and ornate bank area well lit and appealing to the customers. That day the sun had been bright, creating heat and light for those working hard behind the counters. The sun was slowly making its descent, but the light was still bright through the glass.

John G. Mitchell was the president of the bank. He had waved good-bye and headed home a few minutes before the airship had burst into flames in order to catch a train to his suburban home in Cary, Illinois. The building itself was two stories tall and there was no one inside now who was not an employee of the bank. Nothing appeared out of the ordinary until a shadow suddenly fell across the great skylight. Several workers had enough time to look up only to see the skylight explode into pieces and then burning hell fell on top of them.

The engines were heavier than the rest of the debris and they fell through first. Glass rained down on the employees below. They were all standing in a cage meant to keep people out, as the glass and debris from the airship fell on them. They had nowhere to go and they were helpless. First the glass fell, cutting them, tearing open skin and creating huge puddles of blood on the floor. Then came the engines themselves.

The engines had been filled with more fuel than was really necessary for the trip it was destined to make. Thus, when the engines came crashing through the skylight they were nearly filled with fuel. As the engines fell, they had caught fire from the burning hydrogen and had turned into plummeting balls of flame. They crashed to the marble floor and the fuel exploded onto the employees and all over the equipment on the floor. The fuel caught fire and, almost immediately, set the employees ablaze. The air within the bank filled with screams as clothing and skin turned black and charred.

There were nearly 150 employees in the bank building when the blimp crashed through. Most of them were inside the cage. Most of them were women. With the skylight shattered, there was a chimney effect created and the flames were fanned and pulled upward. The gasoline was still spreading across the floor, filling the lobby with burning liquid. The entire floor area of the bank erupted in chaos. The screams echoed off of the marble walls and floors. People ran everywhere and several shoved furniture or fellow co-workers out of the way to get to safety.

On the second floor employees looked down to see their friends burning and the entire first floor turn into a burning inferno. Several employees jumped out of windows to the ground below. Others leaped over railings to the floor below in hopes of pulling people out of the flames or putting out the fire.

As the bank burned so did the rest of the airship. The men inside the gondola had jumped out of the burning ship and opened their chute, except for one. Earl Davenport hadn't been able to make it out of the gondola. He fell into the rooftop of the bank building. When the gondola hit, it hit so forcefully that he was flung from the gondola. Later, after the fire was out and workers found the debris on the roof they found his body buried in the roof. His legs had gone through the roof while the upper half of this body was still sticking out of the roof.

For the rest of those who had jumped, it was no guarantee that they would be safe just because they had a parachute. Carl Weaver had jumped and his parachute had opened right when it was supposed to. However, no sooner had the parachute opened when he looked up to see that the airship was crashing directly on top of him. Witnesses on the ground said they saw him twisting frantically, trying to get out of the way, and he managed not to get hit by the engines, but the fiery outer skin passed right by his thin and very flammable parachute. The chute and his clothing caught fire and soon Carl Weaver was a burning ball just as much as the airship itself had been. His body fell through the broken skylight and crashed to the burning marble floor, all but unnoticed by the screaming employees. Since his body was burned beyond recognition in the flames from his clothes and then the fire in the bank, it was never determined if he died from impact or the flames, but witnesses say he was probably dead from the fire, burned alive while falling.

The streets around the bank had been filled with commuters heading home. Now a crowd began to form, clogging the streets around the bank, as the fire department tried to make their way toward the inferno that the bank had become. The crowd swelled to an estimated 20,000 people.

The firehouses located all around the Loop were rung as the building blazed and the screams of those burning alive filled the air inside and outside the bank. The firemen arrived quickly and they soon had hoses strung and hooked up all around the bank. Water began to pour from the nozzles, but there was so much fuel and it was burning so intensely, the firemen couldn't get close to the building for some time. Slowly, eventually, the fire departments began to put out the flames and they were able to get closer to put out the actual fire in thirty minutes. However, once they got inside, a nightmare greeted them.

The firemen found the mangled remains of the gondola and they began cooling the metal down to start to remove it. From beneath the metal they found twisted bodies, most of them charred beyond recognition. The bodies crumbled beneath the hands of the firemen as they pulled the bodies from the wreckage.

As the gondola had fallen, it began to pull the burning skin with it. The entire airship was now laying burned and broken on the floor, covering the furniture and the people around it. They began removing the still-hot debris and they kept unearthing bodies. There were so many that they decided to send all of them to nearby hospitals. So, stretchers were loaded with smoking bodies and heaped into ambulances and carted off to the nearest hospital that happened to be Iroquois Memorial Hospital, which was soon overwhelmed and had to shut down its emergency room and send the patients elsewhere. (The Iroquois was named after the famous theater fire which had happened not too long before this one.)

The bank building itself had managed to survive the intense fire remarkably well. It had lost people and equipment, but the marble had only blackened. In fact, the bank would be back in business the very next day.

While the people inside the bank were burning alive, the other men, besides Weaver, were also dying. The reporter, William Davenport, had grabbed his bulky camera and the plates he had taken and then jumped. He clutched his camera and plates to his chest as he fell and looked up to see the flaming debris coming right for him. He reached up with one hand and began yanking and twisting the lines of his parachute, moving himself out of the way of the flames. His efforts were feeble because he refused to drop his camera and plates. He succeeded, instead, of getting his parachute caught on the Western Union building and he was smashed against the side. It was then that his camera and plates fell from his hands and he followed suit shortly thereafter. Both of his legs were broken and he was bleeding internally. His body would be found and he would be placed into the hospital and hang on for at least a day. Eventually, however, the internal injuries would be too much for him and he would succumb never knowing that the plates and camera had been smashed to pieces against the ground, but asking about them until the very end.

It was Norton who was able to provide some information about the crash, but no one was really ever sure. Norton spoke with authorities the night before he died. He claimed that he saw flames suddenly from behind him. He stated he just jumped once he saw the flames and he figured the ship was lost. He held tight to his plates and his camera and then tried to guide his parachute. Others on the ground said they saw flames near the front of the airship, not the back as Norton claimed. Other witnesses just said they saw the flames spread and then the entire ship jackknifed and fell.

The pilot, Boettner, was able to control his parachute and his descent to some extent. He later told investigators that he found himself falling rapidly and looked up to see that his parachute had caught fire. He began to spin and whirl wildly and then he was stunned suddenly when he stopped. He claimed he lost consciousness for a few moments, and when he came to, he realized he was on a roof. He was looking down at the street. He stood up and found the fire escape and made his way down to the street. Once he was at street level, he was taken by detectives who had already arrived to investigate the accident.

The last of the Goodyear mechanics, Weaver, was also able to guide his parachute. Where he landed, however, was not mentioned in the stories. It is known that, like Boettner, he was nearly uninjured.

Thirteen employees from the bank were dead and twenty-six were seriously injured. The bank itself was actually more undamaged than anyone could realize. The president of the bank arrived at his station in the suburbs only to be told what had happened at his bank. A train heading the other way had been held up to return him to the city and he did. Most of the uninjured employees of the bank actually returned that night and began cleaning, washing the huge pools of blood away, patching the roof and cleaning up the burned equipment. Neighboring banks pitched in and donated adding machines and typewriters and equipment so the bank could open the next day.

The bank held five minutes of silence the next morning and then opened the doors as normal. The bank was back to normal within weeks and the employees who had survived all returned to work. It was business as usual.

But What Happened?

An inquest was started into the crash. Exactly why the ship exploded was never determined. However, Chicago's plans to become a "blimpopolis" were over. In fact, just that morning a report by aviation experts had been released declaring that airships were the wave of the future and that Chicago was ripe for becoming the Midwest center for airship travel. Just after the *Wingfoot* crashed, state and city officials stepped forward with plans to prevent air traffic from going directly over the city.

The Goodyear company reacted with amazing speed and compassion. They set up funds to pay families of those who had died. They also paid out more money to take care of medical expenses for those who were injured. The company publicly declared that those who were unhappy with their commissions payments could sue for more in court.

The airship had been inspected several times that day. Each time it had been declared safe and air-worthy. The colonel who had been on the airship that day declared that if the ship had not been sound, he would not have flown and his experience with flying gave him credibility for investigators.

Goodyear also declared that the ship had been sound and safe. They released a statement stating that air travel via airship was still safe. Despite the shaky record of airships even at that time, it would take a few decades before the airships would fade entirely.

The story of the *Wingfoot Air Express* would fade from the papers and the national news very quickly. The debate over air traffic over the city would also die down. Eventually, years down the road, the air traffic over the city would be restricted or banned. The problem was that the story itself would be dwarfed by other stories and be all but forgotten by the media and the city itself.

Chapter Thirteen

The Worst Tornado Disaster in Northern Illinois

The Midwest may not technically be in the meteorological area known as "tornado alley" but it does get its share of the monstrous storms. Throughout the history, great Midwestern cities, such as Chicago and St. Louis, are littered with tornado stories. Chicago gets very few tornadoes within the city limits, but there have been plenty in and around it. When there *have* been tornadoes within the city limits, the disasters have been particularly grim and terrible.

One of those times happened in early spring of 1967. April 21, 1967 was one of the worst cases of air taking its vengeance on a city, and unfortunately, many of the victims were children.

The winter of 1966 and into 1967 had been very brutal, which is not particularly rare for the Chicago area. That winter set records with a massive 23-inch snowstorm on January 26th and 27th that shut down the city. The total for that winter was 68.4 inches of snow. From January 26th through March, there was a continuous covering of snow on the ground. Then, as if a switch had been thrown, when spring arrived, the hot weather crashed into an area still recovering from the snow and cold.

During the weekend before the tornado hit, the air temperature in Chicago was in the seventies. During that week, the city of Rockford, about ninety miles northwest of Chicago, had a day where the air temperature reached eighty. Most Chicagoans were smiling, however, certain that this meant a mild spring and some kind of reward for surviving such a horrific winter. They were looking forward to a warm spring and a hot summer.

April 21st was a Friday. After all of those days of warm weather, the atmosphere over most of northern Illinois was unstable. There was a strong west-southwest upper level jet stream stretching from the southwestern U.S. to the Great Lakes. With that jet stream in place, a number of other meteorological situations also happened that made that day particularly dangerous. The air was ripe for storms to form and those storms were likely to be whoppers. By the afternoon, the air was perfect for a line of thunderstorms to form just west and north of Chicago.

The warm front marched through Illinois all afternoon, producing storms throughout the day. Before the storms hit the Belvidere area, right near Rockford, the storm's system had already produced twelve tornadoes. The National Weather Service issued a tornado warning at 1:50 p.m.

The skies over Belvidere began to darken just after three o'clock. It had been warm but stormy all day long. Schools throughout the area were preparing to send the students home. At Belvidere High School a line of school buses stood outside the school filled with elementary school kids, they were now waiting for their daily cargo of high school students. Although the skies were stormy and the wind was blowing and thunder was cracking in the distance, the teachers and officials at the school decided it was best to let the students go in hopes of getting them home before the storms hit.

Roaring Twisters

The first twister touched down at 3:50 p.m. The tornado hit near the area known at Cherry Valley. The massive tornado passed the Chrysler plant just near I-90. As the twister roared through, it wiped out 300 new cars and 100 employee cars. Still the twister continued eastward and entered the town of Belvidere. It headed right for the homes located there, destroying nearly 127 homes. Before it was done, it was recorded as an F4 on the Fujita scale.

The horror in Belvidere came when the tornado hit the high school. Many students were still filing out of the school and getting on the buses. The buses were close to capacity, however. They looked on in horror as the twister bore down on them. Twelve buses stood in a line and the huge twister hit it full on. The twelve buses were tossed about like toys and students were flung across the street into the muddy field located there. Of the 24 Belvidere deaths that day, 13 of them were at the high school. Nearly 300 of the 500 injured were also from the high school.

The tornado continued on into McHenry County. No sooner did the original tornado die out than the storm system spawned another tornado near Woodstock, Illinois. The two tornadoes were, at one point, destroying everything in front of them in a path twenty-five miles wide.

Another F4 tornado was spawned at 5:05 p.m. This one hit the area known as Fox River Grove. Fortunately, this area was largely unpopulated and filled with trees over soft rolling hills. One person was killed, but 75 homes were destroyed. Another 200 homes had extensive damage due to the twister. It hit Fox River Grove, North Barrington, and Lake Zurich. The main thing learned here was that the storm was not producing a visible twister and many could not see the tornado until it was directly on top of them.

The worst part of the storm was approaching the southwestern suburbs of Chicago by 5 p.m. The highways and roads were jammed with cars as workers tried to make their way home after a long day at work. At the weather bureau in Joliet, an employee looked out the window and saw a huge rotating cloud. Shortly thereafter, the funnel was reported to the bureau. The tornado made an official touch down at 88th Avenue just inside Cook County. One of those rare instances where a tornado happened within the city limits was about to occur.

The first homes hit were near 83rd Avenue. The twister then crossed the Tri-State Tollway and plowed into more homes near Harlem Avenue. It then crashed straight into a drive-in movie theater near an area known as Chicago Ridge. It was then that the tornado moved into the heart of Oak Lawn.

The funnel cloud and rotating winds was a city block wide by this time. It began leveling homes entirely, tearing them from their foundations, and leaving just empty basements behind it. The area was soon covered with debris. Once again, this storm created a tornado that seemed hell bent on hitting a school.

The tornado hit a bus garage, sending buses and equipment throughout the neighborhood. One bus crashed through the roof of a house. At this point the twister, having spent so much of its energy on the high school and the bus garage, lost a little of its intensity, only to gain more strength a few moments later. This time it hit a mobile home park and then leveled a roller skating rink. Up next was St. Mary's Cemetery.

The twister plucked the tombstones like flowers being picked by a small girl and it tossed them aside. It ran through the Beverly Hills Country Club and then tore trees out of the

Dan Ryan Woods. After that, it was on a line for a place filled with people. The highways and intersections in that area were packed with cars stuck in traffic. As the frightened motorists looked on, a huge twisting cloud almost completely obscured by rain and debris bore down upon them.

The twister hit the Dan Ryan Expressway, filled with cars and flipped a semi. Debris scattered across the highway, closing that major artery for hours. Cars were sent flying into the sky, ending up scattered across the highway and on houses nearby. Due to this hit, the tornado that ripped through Oak Lawn became the deadliest of that outbreak.

The Aftermath

At the intersection of Southwest Highway and W. 95th Street, the tornado plowed into a glut of cars. After the tornado departed the area, left behind was a pile of destroyed cars and 16 dead. Once it crossed over the expressway, the tornado moved, finally, out over the tip of Lake Michigan. Their it finally lost power and eventually dissipated.

The tornado that tore up the south side of the city and through Oak Lawn killed 33 people. It also knocked down 152 homes and damaged 900. There were 1,000 people injured, scattered to various area hospitals. The total cost of that one tornado was $50 million.

The tornadoes that ripped through the area were part of an outbreak that hit much of northern Illinois. It also hit areas in Missouri, Iowa and Michigan. By the time the outbreak ended there had been 19 tornadoes and 58 people were dead.

Just as the city of Chicago started to clean up the spring-like weather notorious in Chicago, weather struck again. Two days later a snowstorm hit and dumped three inches of snow over the area. This prevented those trying to clean up the area wrecked by the tornado as the temperatures plummeted. The governor declared a state of emergency for much of the area affected and even the Illinois reserves stepped in to assist with the clean-up efforts.

It was easily one of the worst tornadoes and storms to hit the Chicago area. However, even more sadly, it would not be the last. No, the city of air had even greater disasters in store for the citizens and those on the ground around it.

Chapter Fourteen

Flight 553

Chicago may not have become a place for blimps and airships, but it has certainly become a major hub for air travel. This came into play when planes took over as the major form of transportation sometime after World War I. While these days Chicago is most famous for O'Hare International Airport, located on the northwest side of the city, there was a time when Chicago's second major airport was one of the busiest in the world. This airport exists today and is still active and busy despite having long ago lost its title as busiest in the world. This airport is known as Midway Airport.

Midway is located on the south side of the city. It is surrounded, on all sides, by homes and neighborhoods. Busy roads run on all sides as well. It is like having a major airport sitting in your backyard and the planes come in low over those rooftops all day and all night long.

When airplanes used propellers to get into the air and fly, Midway was the perfect size to handle the traffic. During the fifties, and even slightly earlier, when major commercial airlines were still in their infancy and much of the world still saw traveling by air as a novelty, the fields of Midway Airport became the center of traffic for the country. However, when planes got larger and turned to jet propulsion, the smaller runways at Midway became insufficient. O'Hare was built and became the major hub that it is today.

Eventually, however, Midway's runways were adapted to handle the larger jets. However, there was only so far that the runways could expand before they just ran out of space. Without wanting to completely destroy old neighborhoods around the airport, Midway was always going to be a little limited in the amount of traffic and size of the planes it could handle. While it remains a major hub, it never has regained the prominence it once held.

In 1972, a great deal of the heyday of Midway was over. However, jets were taking off and landing at the airport regularly, the loud machines roaring what seemed like feet over the rooftops of the surrounding neighborhoods. Flight 553, on an airplane with the name *City of Lincoln*, was supposed to be making a flight to Omaha, Nebraska, with a brief stop at Chicago's Midway Airport. The plane was a 737.

An Important Flight

While flights in and out of the airport had long ago become routine, this was not just a routine flight. On board was Illinois Congressman George W. Collins. To make things more intriguing, the wife of the future Watergate conspirator E. Howard Hunt, Dorothy Hunt, was also on the plane. Michele Clark was a fairly well-known correspondent for *CBS News* and she was on board as well. Clark was one of the very first African-American female correspondents for the network. Finally, a well-known and respected ophthalmologist, Alex E. Krill, was also flying on that 737.

It was winter again in the Windy City. The date was December 8th and the flight was standard as it left Washington National Airport. It approached the city over the Lake and headed in for runway 31L after being told which runway to go to by the tower dispatcher. At some point, the tower informed the plane to abort its first attempt at landing and to circle around and try again. The plane headed back into the air and began to circle around.

Inside the cockpit were three crew members. Although the 737 had been built to be handled by only two crew members, the pilot's union contract at that time stipulated that all United Airlines flights had to have a three-man crew. The plane was not full, but did have a full flight attendant crew.

The plane pulled up and struck trees located in the neighborhoods surrounding the airport. Then, to the horror of those on the ground, tower, and plane, the plane hit rooftops. Shortly after, the plane went down and into a house. The house was located in the 3700 block of West 70th Place. As the neighborhoods were catapulted into shock and terror, others in the area came outside to see what the chaos was. A ball of fire flew into the air and the sound of the plane crashing echoed throughout the neighborhood.

When the smoke had cleared, there were forty-five people dead. Forty-three of them died on the plane. The entire crew inside the cockpit died. One flight attendant near the front of the plane survived when her jump seat collapsed. Although severely injured, she was alive. Fifteen other passengers survived. Two more flight attendants also survived, but all of the surviving passengers and attendants were located in coach. The remaining two deaths were in the house.

Investigation

At the time, this crash was the most investigated in history. One of the biggest controversies and issues that had to be investigated turned out to be the death of Hunt's wife. Her purse, it was discovered, had $10,585 inside it. To add to the mystery, she had purchased flight insurance in the amount of $250,000 just prior to boarding the flight. Before too long the conspiracy theorists came out of the woodwork and began to suggest that government agencies were responsible for bringing the plane down. As the National Transportation Safety Board (NTSB) investigated the crash, the FBI suddenly stepped in as rumors of the plane being sabotaged began to grow and become more persistent.

In a *Time* magazine interview with one of President Nixon's chief administrators, and suspect in the growing Watergate Scandal, stated he felt that the CIA had murdered Dorothy Hunt. Those within the CIA then charged that Nixon and his staff were merely trying to distract from the investigation and growing public outcry over the growing scandal. Since several administrators, including the one interviewed for the article, were facing prison sentences and Nixon was staring at a possible impeachment, the idea that the conspiracy was merely smoke appears to have validity.

The NTSB made some suspicious discoveries. They found that the Flight Data Recorder had stopped working about fourteen minutes before the plane crashed. Thus, some critical data that would have sped the investigation was lost. However, radar tapes stored within the control tower at Midway Airport were undamaged and they showed the track and airspeed of the flight as well as other critical data. The cockpit voice recorder was also still functioning and timed with the radar data. It was shown that the stick shaker had started to go off six or seven seconds after the plane had leveled off when it reached 1,000 feet. It was determined that this continued to go off until the plane crashed and it ceased to function. (A "stick-shaker" is a control on an airplane that is connected with an alarm and sensor. It causes the "stick" or the mechanism the pilot and co-pilot hold to control the plane, to shake and vibrate violently. It does this when the plane senses that they are turning the plane too hard and thus they are likely to cause an engine stall.)

The stick shaker was meant to go off when the plane was about to stall. Thus, it became evident that the pilot, upon pulling up and attempting to abort the landing, had failed to achieve the necessary airspeed to pull off the maneuver. This had caused the engines to stall and the plane had lost altitude and crashed.

The plane had been flying too high and too fast upon its initial approach. The Captain had control of the plane when attempting the first landing. There was poor coordination and training among the cockpit crew and the Captain decided to continue the landing even though he was 700 feet too high at a critical point during that first landing attempt. He still attempted the landing and realized, too late, that he was too fast and too high and called for thrust to attempt to fly back around. It was too little, too late.

The damaged plane was examined extensively. Every component of the plane was studied and analyzed under both NTSB and FBI surveillance. No evidence of sabotage was ever found and "pilot error" was the ultimate decision of those investigating.

Despite having more people than needed to fly the plane, the crew had horribly misjudged the landing and the proper procedures for pulling out of the landing and flying around. The flaps were wrong and so were wing extensions known as "spoilers." Neither the Captain nor the rest of the crew noticed these errors and failed to correct them which helped precipitate the crash.

Midway Airport still operates. There are still houses circling the airfield. Planes continue to take off and land what seems like mere feet above homes of entire families. Despite this, the airport has a remarkable safety record. There was not another disaster at this airport until, on almost the same day, a plane attempting to land during a severe snowstorm, overshot the runway, and slid through a fence and into traffic, crushing a car and killing a small boy.

As long as planes continue to take off and land in and around airports, there will likely continue to be tragedies like this. In fact, it was only a matter of time before a crash was likely to happen at O'Hare International Airport. It would turn out to be one of the worst in the history of the country.

Chapter Fifteen

The DC-10

By the time 1979 rolled around, the city of Chicago was a major hub when it came to air transportation. Early in its history (as mentioned prior), the airport known as Midway was the busiest airport in the world. This was a title it held for some time, but during the sixties, it was decided to turn a large empty field into an airport named after a World War II flying ace named "Butch" O' Hare.

Before too long the air traffic had shifted to O'Hare, and not long after that, it became an international airport, with planes flying in from all over the world and sending people all over the world. While the city had never become the "blimpopolis" it was once promised to be at the turn of the century, as jets took over the air traffic, it had certainly become a major center for that kind of travel.

Ever day, hundreds of planes took off and landed at O'Hare Airport on the northwest side of town. This airport, too, was surrounded by neighborhoods and businesses. The entire airport was connected to the city by a single strip of highway known as the Kennedy Expressway.

On May 25, 1979, the day couldn't have been brighter, sunnier, or fairer for those hoping to travel via air. The day was warm, but not overly so. It was still spring and, at any moment, the air was likely to shift off the Lake and turn the air cold. The airport had become the major hub for a couple of the major airlines. American Airlines used O'Hare almost exclusively and United Airlines also used the airport as its hub. The airport was now the busiest in the entire world with only airports like Atlanta or Moscow close behind.

The mainstay airplane of the airline industry had become the DC-10. The plane had become a true workhorse, used by most of the airlines, criss-crossing the skies and transporting people across the country. The plane was considered as advanced as it could be and one of the safest in the air. The plane was also large and reliable with room for over 200 passengers.

Flight 191

That afternoon Flight 191 was scheduled to fly from Chicago to Los Angeles International Airport. The plane had been in service for eight years, having been delivered to American Airlines in 1972. The plane had 20,000 hours of flight by the time May 25th came around. It waited at the gates that afternoon, glinting in the sun, with the wind slow at about 22 knots. In the terminal, 271 people waited to board the plane and make the trip to the West Coast. All around them planes were pulling away from the gates and flying off to various destinations. More planes were landing and spitting out their loads of passengers into the terminal.

The captain of the flight was Walter Lux at the age of fifty-three and a man with years of experience in the air. The man flying next to him was James Dillard, who was forty-nine. The engineer for the flight was Alfred Udovich and he was fifty-six years of age. Lux had nearly 22,000 hours in the air. The other two men had 25,000 hours of flight time between them. Behind the flight deck were the usual compliment of ten flight attendants. All of them were prepared for a smooth flight in clear weather. In short, it was a routine day for them and they expected nothing out of the ordinary.

Everything about the plane was declared safe and ready for take-off. The engines and the fuselage had been inspected and deemed okay. The flight crew checked and double-checked their pre-flight checklists. All seemed fine. Sometime after two that afternoon, the passengers were lined up at the gate and their tickets were checked. The passengers walked down the ramp, eagerly waiting for the plane to streak into the sky and take them to Los Angeles. Many of those on the flight were part of Chicago's literary community and headed to LA for a convention.

Just before three that afternoon, Flight 191 was cleared to pull away from the gate. It was told to head toward runway 32R. Slowly, the plane headed toward the runway, trundling along the ground, waiting for other planes to take off. The plane moved slowly, the flight crew in constant communication with the tower. The passengers gazed out the windows as the airport passed by their windows and then behind them. By 3:02 the flight had been cleared for takeoff and the plane stood at the end of runway 32R.

What happened next was one of the worst airline disasters in United States history. In fact, to this day, it stands as the worst *accidental* airplane crash.

The accident happened very fast. For those on the plane, it must have seemed like an eternity. For those on the ground it was one of the most terrifying spectacles they had ever seen. What no one knew was that a series of small errors in preparing the plane had doomed those on board Flight 191 even before it revved its engines to attempt a takeoff.

The DC-10 trembled as the engines roared into life, building and building to deafening heights. Then it began to trundle down the runway. There were thousands of feet of runway to cover. The one person with the best view of what happened next was working in the control tower. After covering about 6,000 feet of runway the air-traffic controller saw the left engine break off of the wing, hit the runway and then bounce over the wing and the aircraft. With a crash, the engine and the mountings that held it to the wing crashed down on the tarmac.

Inside the control deck the pilots tried to figure out what had happened. Cockpit recordings show that they were unsure of exactly what had happened. When the engine sheered away it severed the hydraulic lines, leaving the pilots with no control. The pilots still thought they could ascend and make a return landing. They fought the airplane, lifting to about 350 feet over the runway. Then, inexorably they lost control and the plan tilted violently to the left, nearly flipping upside down. At this point, a famous photograph showing the plane tipped to the side was snapped and ended up in the newspapers and on the news all over the country in the next few days.

The plane made it out over the end of the runway and across Touhy Avenue, a major thoroughfare that ran past the airport. Across the street from the airport was a trailer park. Next to the trailer park was a series of huge oil tanks, filled to near capacity. Between the two was a field.

The pilots tried to reduce their speed to 165 knots. With the hydraulic lines severed, this proved to be impossible. When the lines had been severed, most of the controls that would have alerted the pilots to the exact conditions of the airplane had also been severed. One important device, known as a stick shaker, was only on the pilot's controls and it was no longer functioning. Had the stick shaker been on the co-pilot's side as well, he might have known that the plane was in greater danger than they realized and would have been able to react more properly.

The plane eventually stalled as the pilots continued to reduce their air speed. It soon fell below the buildings of the airport. The entire time the plane had been in the air amounted to about 31 seconds. As the plane fell it clipped a hangar of the old Ravenswood Airport.

The plane crashed into the ground hard enough to drive a furrow into the ground. The fuselage plowed into the unused field which was owned by a construction site. The engines were full of jet fuel and soon there was a huge fireball roiling and boiling up into the sky, spreading burning fuel and fire across the field. The fireball was so huge that people in buildings downtown could see it easily. The aircraft exploded and broke into pieces. The pieces also scattered across the field and some of the burning fuel and debris hit a small building used by the construction company, killing two workers inside. The entire crew and all of the passengers were killed nearly instantly with the impact and explosion. With that, 271 people on board the plane died, which was everyone on board.

On the Ground

The cockpit voice recorder was powered by the severed engine. There was a recording of the pilot saying "damn" and then nothing. Inside the control tower the controllers went into a panic. They could only look on in horror as the plane went down. Several times the controllers attempted to contact Flight 191 to see if they could assist, but they got no response. When it became obvious that the plane was going down the immediately called for emergency services and declared an emergency.

Other witnesses around the airport were visited by the press and gave their reports. The media arrived in full force and began covering the fire and the recovery effort. The fire department arrived and began evacuating residents from the mobile home park. They also began trying to fight the fire. The jet fuel was burning furiously and with such intense heat that they couldn't get close enough to fight the fire.

At that time, American Airlines would let passengers watch their planes take off from closed circuit televisions. It is unknown if the passengers on Flight 191 were able to see their own plane crashing or not, however. An amateur photographer caught the famous shot of the plane tipping to one side and the picture was the banner of the *Chicago Tribune* the next morning. Another man, filming planes taking off and landing, caught the entire thing on his home film camera.

Area hospitals were put on red alert to treat any survivors. Not long after the fire department reached the site of the crash, however, it became evident that no one was going to survive this crash. The entire city stood still and in front of televisions or near radios for the live coverage of the crash and fire.

For days, the coverage of the crash dominated the local Chicago media. The newspapers were filled with images of firefighters walking through the field and the wreckage, marking spots where bodies or body parts were found. Meanwhile the NTSB swung into action to try and figure out exactly what had happened and why.

Why it Happened

The first controversy was that this was now the fourth fatal DC-10 crash in recent memory. Since they had come into existence and become the industry workhorse, nearly 622 people had died in fatal airline disasters involving DC-10s. Since the weather had been so perfect and radar signatures and checking the engines revealed that a flock of birds had not hit the aircraft, the airplane itself was called into question. The media seized upon this and, before long, both the media and the public were calling for the removal of DC-10s from service.

Misinformation began coming from the crash site. First, there was a rumor that a small plane had hit the aircraft. This turned out to be parts of a plane scattered about the field when the airliner had struck the airplane hangar. When reports from the air traffic controller, who had witnessed the crash, surfaced saying he thought he had seen a flash from the wing just before the engine separated fueled rumors of a terrorist bomb.

At some point, investigators looking through the debris, thought they had found the cause of the problem. Since the engine had been clearly seen falling off of the plane before it took off, the focus of the investigation was there. A member of the investigating team made an announcement to the press that an improperly made bolt had been the cause of the entire accident. Since other DC-10s also used the same kind of bolt, this sent a panic through the traveling world and more calls were made to remove DC-10s from active service. Eventually the FAA and NTSB would recommend that all DC-10s be taken out of service and inspected as continued investigations revealed that there were flaws with the design of the aircraft.

It turned out that a single bolt could not have been the cause of the crash. In fact, the engine falling off alone should not have been enough to bring down the aircraft. However, when the engine and the pylon that held it to the wing went, it ripped out vital electrical and hydraulic lines that prevented the pilots from reacting properly, which was ultimately what brought the plane down.

It turned out that improper maintenance procedures had doomed the plane eight weeks before that fateful day. When the plane had been taken to the Tulsa maintenance facility, the engine had been removed. It had been recommended by the company that built the plane, McDonnell-Douglas, that the engine and the pylon attaching it to the wing be removed as two separate units to prevent damage. American Airlines, along with some other airlines, had created an unapproved method of removing the engine and pylon as one unit to save time.

The procedure occurred like this: A large forklift was brought in and the forks placed beneath the wing and pylon. The pylon and engine would be removed and placed on the forklift and held near its original placement during the removal process. This was a very precise and difficult undertaking, often done in a hurry and without all procedures and safety in mind. This method of removal allowed for the engines and pylons to become more easily damaged. Several other planes and engines were found to have damage when they were inspected upon being removed from service, as well.

Damage

At the Tulsa facility, the procedure for removal for the plane that would become Flight 191 did not go smoothly. The forklift was in the wrong position and the engine rocked and moved as it was removed, driving it against the pylon and the attachment points on the wing. In the middle of the removal process, a shift change also occurred, which caused further confusion and problems. When the new shift arrived, the engine and pylon was jammed beneath the wing and the entire assembly plus the forklift had to be repositioned. This caused the assembly to ram against the underside of the wing, causing further damage to where the pylon and engine would connect to the wing.

The damage was small, but ultimately fatal. The pin assembly that held the engine on was damaged. The housing that held the pin was also damaged. This weakened the entire engine and pylon assembly. The stress of the plane going back into service caused the weakened points to form stress fractures. In short, it was only a matter of time before a disaster was likely to happen. When Flight 191 had generated all of that thrust and rocketed down the runway, this created enough force to rip the entire assembly off the plane and doom it as well.

Still, other planes, including DC-10s, had lost engines and been able to make safe return landings. As such, just losing the engine should not have been enough to cause Flight 191 to crash. The hydraulic lines being cut caused parts of the wings that can be extended, known as slats, to retract when they needed to be extended. The DC-10 had two hydraulic lines which should have prevented the loss of one to cause a loss of the plane. However, the way the plane was designed, those two lines were very close together, so Flight-191 lost both when the engine and pylon tore away.

The engine tearing away also caused electrical equipment to become non-functional. The voice recorder, for example, no longer functioned. The slat warning system no longer worked. Therefore, no one in that flight deck could know if the slats were extended or not. They were flying a crippled aircraft without having a way to properly identify its condition. Studies of the flight showed that the pilots, with the knowledge they had, did attempt to fly the plane properly. However, there was no way they could have known just how badly damaged their aircraft was, that the slats had retracted, or that they should not have reduced speed as they did. All of their training told them otherwise.

However, even that was not enough. There were warning systems that should have alerted the pilots to the fact that they were reducing speed to a dangerous stall level. However, those electronics were also in the wing and near the engine. They were ripped away as well when the engine and pylon tore away. This included the pilot's stick shaker, which would have been his indication that he was nearing a stall speed. American Airlines had gone with the pilot-side-only stick shaker when they first ordered the planes, not knowing that it would contribute to one of the worst disasters in American history.

The pilots did the best they could, it was determined. There was just too much going against them once the engine and pylon had torn away. The problems truly began with the maintenance procedure in Tulsa. Then, in the air, when the plane went sideways and the engine stalled, there was no way to save the aircraft and Flight 191 was truly doomed.

DC-10s were taken from the skies for much of 1979. Other planes were found with stress fractures. More DC-10s were found with other flaws and problems. It was determined that a more safe and efficient DC-10 was the answer to the problem rather than switching to a different aircraft all together.

McDonnell-Douglas suffered because of this. The company tried to combat the negative publicity. Employees even held an "I'm proud of the DC-10" campaign that had little affect calming the public. The stock of the company fell by more than twenty percent after the crash. This was actually unfair as the aircraft itself was sound, but cost cutting maintenance procedures were often the real reason for DC-10 accidents.

O'Hare Airport continued to be the busiest in the world for many years to come. It would eventually relinquish that title to Atlanta. Mayor Daley ultimately campaigned for O'Hare to expand and increase the number of runways available, and to increase the air traffic the airport was able to handle.

The crash killed many members of the Chicago literary and publishing community. There were also several close calls such as the pop band Shoes who were scheduled to be on the flight but switched at the last minute due to scheduling problems. The actress Lindsey Wagner also had a ticket for that flight but felt uneasy about it and changed at the last minute as well.

These days, ghost stories abound as well in the area near where the plane crashed. Residents in the mobile home park claim they hear noises, see lights in the empty field or run across strange people in outdated clothing wandering the field or within the park itself. Some claim that they have found people looking confused at their doors and invited them in only to see them disappear.

No one knows if any of that is true, of course. What is known is that on a bright and sunny day, a plane filled with people fell from the skies over Chicago. It left the city stunned, changed the way planes were maintained throughout the world, nearly brought down a major corporation, and changed the way DC-10s were thought of in the minds of the public for a long time to come.

Chapter Sixteen

Disaster in Plainfield

In northern Illinois, on August 28, 1990, the weather forecast called for "little change, with some rain and a little cooler temperatures." Although August can be a very hot and humid month for the Chicago area, by the end of the month, as the weeks slowly turned into September, the month becomes cooler. In 1990, however, it was hot and humid even that late in the month.

The normal temperature for that time of year is around 79 degrees. The days around August 28th, the air temperatures had been in the high 80s and even into the 90s. On August 28, the air temperature had reached into the low 90s, while the dew points reached into the upper 70s. The day before, the weather had been similar and there was little to indicate that there was a chance for thunderstorms that day.

However, as the day began to wear on, the heat caused the air to become unstable. Upper and mid-level air disturbances began to weave their way through the area as well and the air became more and more unstable. By the time the afternoon arrived, the air was perfect for thunderstorms and the National Weather Service issued a Severe Thunderstorm Watch.

The National Severe Storms Forecast Center issued that first warning and predicted that it would last until 8 p.m. The organization predicted that storms would likely form that evening as a cold front swept down from the Wisconsin border and across northern Illinois. However, the storms began to form much earlier than predicted and rain showers began to crop up along the Illinois-Wisconsin border.

When a storm build and builds reaching severe levels and then begins to show signs of rotation, this is often referred to as a supercell. One of these supercells formed just south and east of Rockford, Illinois, and began heading south and east toward Chicago. It began producing huge sheets of rain, powerful lightning, and nearly continuous thunder.

It also produced a tornado.

Chicago soon felt the edges of this massive storm. The skies to the east and north turned a terrifyingly dark color. The skies turned almost black and the clouds churned, according to witnesses. Torrents of rain began to hammer the city from nearly one end to the other. The storm lasted for hours, pouring buckets of rain and lightning and thunder over the city. Then, suddenly, at about 4:30 p.m., the skies suddenly cleared, the sun came out, and the air became eerily calm. It was then that the tornado touched down.

A Hidden Twister

The storms had already produced at least one tornado. This was a small twister that touched down just after one o'clock. That twister had caused little damage, removing a few roofing tiles and frightening more than a few people, but otherwise doing little. Still, the National Weather Service, overwhelmed as it was with weather reports for much of Illinois and into Missouri, did not issue a tornado warning.

The town of Plainfield in 1990 was a rapidly growing suburb filled with housing and apartment complexes. There was new construction everywhere and new townhomes and condo units going up all over. This area was south and west of Chicago, providing an area where young people could easily afford new homes and condos, could move and live, and still have easy access to Chicago.

The city of Plainfield was growing rapidly. On that day, the residents looked into the darkening skies with concern, but there were no sirens. There were no warnings. In fact, the rain was so intense, there was no visible funnel cloud. The funnel was "rain wrapped" as known by meteorologists. This means that there were sheets of rain getting sucked into the wind and wrapping around the funnel cloud, obscuring it nearly completely.

The tornado touched down in a town called Oswego, Illinois. The winds were high and the storm quickly gathered strength. Before long, it was an F5, the highest level and most destructive tornado on the Fujita scale. The storm then entered Will County, south of the city of Chicago and drove through the Wheatland Plans subdivision. Directly in the crosshairs of the storm was Plainfield. As the storm ripped through Wheatland Plains, it destroyed twelve homes but did not kill anyone.

The time was nearing 3:30 p.m. and the huge storm was still wrapped in rain and preventing anyone from seeing the telltale funnel cloud. The building containing the Plainfield High School was right in the path and the huge storm ripped through the building. Three people inside were killed, including a science teacher and two maintenance workers. Several students who were outside, practicing for the various sports teams, ran into the building and took shelter in a hallway and survived. Once the storm had passed and the wreckage of the school analyzed, that hallway was the only thing left standing.

The storm had lost none of its strength as it headed for the Plainfield School District Administration offices. A secretary was killed as the huge storm tore through the building, leaving more rubble behind and scattering debris for blocks. Up next was St. Mary Immaculate Church and the school attached there. This too was thrown like a toy, and three more people lost their lives.

As the storm destroyed the church, it then moved into the church graveyard and ripped apart tombstones, sending them flying through the air like missiles. Fifty-five homes were destroyed as the storm roared through Plainfield itself. A strip mall and a grocery store were hit.

Then the storm moved southeast headed for the large suburban city of Joliet. The storm tore directly through the downtown area of Joliet, destroying buildings and homes as it went. Homes in Crystal Lawns, Lily Cache, and Warwick were destroyed and five more people lost their lives. The storm continued on, showing a penchant for destroying schools, as it ripped apart the Grand Prairie Elementary School. At the Joliet Mall patrons huddled in doorways and watched as the massive wall of swirling water and debris moved like the finger of God just past the mall.

As the storm moved through the Joliet area, it left sixty-nine homes in Crystal Lawns destroyed. In an area known as Peerless Estates, seventy-five homes were leveled to their foundations. In the area known as Lily Cache there were fifty-five houses wrecked. While in Warwick, an additional fifty houses were gone. In several of the areas, the houses were brand new, having just finished being built.

Up next on the storm's path of destruction was the suburb of Crest Hill. The storm was moving with incredible speed and it was only 3:38 when the tornado hit the Crest Hill Lakes Apartment complex. The wind and storm was still at F5 strength as it hit. The bricks and wood and stone of the complex proved to be no protection and a huge section of the complex was completely ripped apart, sending debris and people into the various fields and open areas around the complex. Eight more people lost their lives as the twister roared through the apartment complex.

The Colony West subdivision was next in the path of the storm. Twelve townhomes, newly built, were destroyed and have never been rebuilt. While in the subdivision, a married couple were in a car that went flying through the air. When it crashed, they were killed.

The storm continued, gradually losing strength now. The twister finally left the ground as it rolled through Woodlawn Avenue and Campbell Street in the town of Joliet. At that point, the twister became a thunderstorm. The winds were still high, though, and the sheets of rain pounded homes and people as the storm continued to move east. It crossed the Indiana border and the entire storm dissipated by 4:30. The storm had ripped a path 16 miles long and caused 140 million dollars worth of damage. Most of the damage was done in a short eight-minute span.

Another Aftermath

The city was stunned. In the eerie aftermath, as the sun finally broke through the clouds and the rain died down, many stood in the wreckage of their homes or helped look for survivors, wondering how this had happened. A tornado warning had not been issued. The sirens had not gone off. The tornado itself had been almost impossible to see. It was like the "Big Bad Wolf" had shown up and blown the houses down just south and west of one of the biggest cities in the country.

Initial studies by meteorologists showed that the area where the tornado had hit experienced a major tornado of F3 or higher ever twelve to fifteen years. Since the Plainfield tornado, there has been no tornado of that magnitude at the time of this writing, although an F1 did hit the area in 2004.

The National Weather Service found itself under heavy criticism after the tornado. They had provided no warning of the impending storm. The analysis showed that the forecasting process inside the Chicago office was severely flawed. Since the office was responsible for providing warnings and watching for the entire state of Illinois, it was determined that the office was overburdened. The office, as investigations had shown, did release a warning at 2:32 which was nearly an hour after the first tornado had been on the ground. When the warning was released, however, there was no indication for anyone about where the tornado was on the ground or where it was headed. There was also a hesitation about releasing the warning by the office.

The National Weather Service declared that the Chicago area had the worst record in the nation. They had unsuccessfully issued warnings for severe storms, and issued warnings only twenty-four percent of the time when a warning was justified. The hesitation was determined to be a fear on the part of the office to release warnings that turned out to be unjustified. This actually became known as the Plainfield Syndrome. It was decided, and became policy, that it was better to issue too many warnings, and be wrong, than not to issue one and end up with a disaster like this one.

The Weather Service then set about easing the workload of the Chicago office. They set up offices in the Quad Cities, St. Louis, Indianapolis and Paducah. Those offices were allowed to issue their own warnings and were set up with their own systems to track storms.

The Plainfield tornado also pushed for the installation of NEXRAD, or next generation radar, to assist meteorologists in recognizing tornadoes much sooner. The new radar gave them a better look into the storms to actually determine the airflows inside and make better predictions. The new radar could also detect wind speeds internally for specific storms and better see the telltale rotation that indicated a tornado. This allowed forecasters to issue thunderstorm and tornado warnings much earlier.

Once again, it took a severe tragedy in Chicago to change the way weather was forecasted throughout the country. It took the deaths of 29 people and 140 million dollars in damages, but improvements were made.

Chapter Seventeen

Heat Wave

The weather in the Midwestern states is a study in opposites. Most people know about the harsh winters with the intense cold that comes barreling out of the north and seems to turn the middle section of the country into a froze wasteland. Most who live in warmer climates know only of the cold in Chicago. To some, it would seem that one could ice skate down Michigan Avenue, dodging polar bears along the way, even when in the middle of July. This is not true, of course.

During the summer months, in particular July and August, the jet stream changes its direction. Instead of pulling cold air from the Arctic like it does during the winter, it pulls warm and hot air out of the south. During July and August, and even into September, the air temperatures soar into the 80s, 90s, and even into the 100s. Combined with this, the stream pulls moisture up from the Gulf of Mexico. This makes the air feel like walking into a wet blanket, increasing the overall discomfort and taking a toll on the human body.

Weather and the human body is a strange thing. Both with cold and heat, there tends to be a cumulative effect on humans. The longer both goes on, the more the body becomes incapable of dealing with the extremes. Crucial systems within the body can start to fail and deaths can occur.

This effect can be seen to even greater effect during hot months. Fortunately, the lake next to the city of Chicago often creates a kind of natural air conditioner. This helps the city keep from frying. However, there are times when even this natural cooling mechanism, as large as it is, can fail and the city bakes.

There is another problem in cities like Chicago—there is a large poor population. This is true in large cities all around the world, of course. These people often live in small apartments that lack even a window-unit air conditioner. If they live in particularly bad neighborhoods, they may not want to open a window, either. So, the small apartments in those buildings soon begin to feel like ovens, and the people sit there, day after day, baking themselves as the temperature inside grows beyond the temperature outside.

The weather every year had grown warm and then hot in Chicago. There have been heat waves before, but the city always felt that the people living in the city could take care of themselves. They had no plan for providing relief for those who could not afford air conditioning. No one seemed to know that providing a few hours of cool relief was enough for a body to continue and survive. Therefore, there were no "cooling centers." There was no plan to check on the poor and elderly.

So, when July of 1995 came, the city was not prepared. The entire Midwest was suddenly in the grip of a heat wave where the temperatures soared above three digits and then stayed there for days on end. On July 12th and running through July 16th, the air temperature was over 100 degrees. On July 13th, a record was set at 106. At night, there was no relief either as the temperature only dropped into the upper 70s or lower 80s. The humidity was relentless, which, combined with the temperature, made the heat index reach temperatures of 119 and 125 during the hottest points of the wave.

When compared to other heat waves that the city had experienced, such as in the 1930s or 1988, or other years, the difference was the humidity. During those years, the heat was generated by bare, hot, and dry soil, or heat that had generated in hot and less-humid areas of the country. In those previous years, there were also days where clouds helped remove some of the heat baking the cement. This was not the case in 1995 when the days were cloudless and there was no relief to be had.

In the heart of the city, where the crime was high and the residents generally poor, the temperature was getting worse and worse. The elderly were soon the first to start becoming victims as they were less likely to open their doors or windows for fear of crime. They were also less likely to have air conditioning or even a fan. They were likely isolated.

At the various city morgues, dead bodies began to show. At first, this was considered just a normal event to coincide with the heat. Every year there were heat-related deaths. Soon, however, to those working in the morgues and hospitals, the heat wave of 1995 was turning into something different. The number of bodies continued to grow and space within the city morgues suddenly began to be used up.

The city was slow to respond. Reporters began to ask questions and the city responded by saying that the deaths were likely not all related to the heat. Just because someone died during a heat wave, it was stated, did not mean the death was directly connected to the heat.

Since the city itself did not acknowledge that the deaths were related to the heat, and it was difficult to determine exactly what deaths were connected with the heat, no accurate records were kept to determine how many people actually died because of the heat wave. Some believe that the total numbered around 600, but there is no official toll.

Looking at city records, during the week of the heat wave, an additional 739 people died above the normal weekly average. When looking at those who died, some interesting statistics were realized. Elderly men were more likely to die than women. This was reasoned that women were prone to cultivate relationships and friendships and more likely to "stay connected" to people who would check on them. Elderly men were more likely to be alone with no one to turn to. More African Americans were expected to die than Caucasians or Hispanics. African Americans, at that time, were often living in sub-standard housing and in less cohesive neighborhoods. Hispanics, meanwhile, might also live in poor housing, but they usually had strong communities and closer families.

Those with pre-existing medical conditions were at higher risk. The heat seemed to affect the old and the young. Those with trouble breathing or heart trouble might also be in danger, suffering or even dying during the heat wave.

Chicago was like a city you would normally find in the tropics. Added to the heat and humidity was the layer of pollution that was pressed down upon the city. The air itself was thick with humidity and pollution. Meanwhile, the city was setting new records for energy usage. Everyone with air conditioning was not only running their conditioners but running them at full blast. This caused some power outages.

In an attempt to find relief, in some areas of the city, people opened up fire hydrants. So many hydrants were opened at once that entire neighborhoods lost water pressure. When emergency crews entered those neighborhoods to close the hydrants, they found themselves dodging bricks, rocks, and angry residents.

The heat was unheard of. The roads began to buckle as the asphalt and pavement literally melted and began to sag. Rails on the train lines warped beneath the cloudless skies and blistering sun. City workers were asked to hose down the cities' bridges to prevent them from locking together as the metal expanded. School buses were generally metal boxes with little in the way of air conditioning; some children became so dehydrated and sick that they had to be watered down by the fired department. The city hospitals became filled with sick children, adults, and the elderly.

The area of the city near the downtown area developed what has been termed an "urban heat island." Essentially, there was cooler air all around, but the air over the city was hotter than anywhere else. This prevented the air from cooling effectively at night. Temperatures at night were more than two degrees hotter than normal. This island effect was caused by the concentration of buildings, glass, and pavement in certain areas. These absorb heat throughout the day and then radiate less during the day, causing them to become hotter and hotter.

The city did not have a plan in place to check on those who might be in distress. There were no warnings issued. There were not enough cooling centers. The city did not issue an excessive heat warning until the very last day of the heat wave. There were so many calls for emergencies that the ambulances were overwhelmed. Fire trucks were often used in place of ambulances.

Eventually, as all weather phenomenon do, the heat wave ended. Cooler air began to filter into the city. Relief was found even in the poorest neighborhoods. The blame game started shortly thereafter. The Medical Examiner began labeling the deaths as heat related, and the city officials began battling with one another over who was to blame. Many made public statements stating that the numbers were elevated and that deaths that had nothing to do with the heat were being classified as heat related.

Despite not taking blame for the deaths, the city took steps to prevent the tragedy from happening again. They called in city planners from areas that deal with heat waves more regularly, such as St. Louis, to provide advice for what the city should do in the future. A program where city workers and emergency workers would travel door to door and check on those who live alone, distributing fans or providing transportation to cooling centers. More cooling centers were opened to provide that relief to those who could not find it at home. Just a few hours in cooler air is enough for the body to recuperate from the cumulative effect of the heat.

The exact death toll will never be known. Some records, it was accused, were changed so that the toll due to the heat would not appear as high. Some suggest that the death toll may have been estimated by 250 less than actually died as many bodies were quickly processed and buried before they could be autopsied.

There have been heat waves since. Some of them have neared the level of 1995. However, none has duplicated the death toll or the damage done. It seems that Chicago, despite acknowledging any fault in the disaster, had again learned from its past.

Part Four

City of Earth

Chicago is a city born from the earth. When the first people saw the area that would become the great city, they saw only a huge field, filled with wild onions. It was this smell that gave the city its name. From that earth came the trading post which became the fort and then the city of stone and glass and metal that stands there now.

The materials used to build those early structures were taken almost directly from the earth. The trees were cut down or uprooted from the ground. The materials eventually used to make bricks came from the soil. Even the elements that make up the iron and steel were buried within the earth.

The earth around Chicago is unique and posed interesting challenges to those who first proposed building some of the nation's fire skyscrapers. The builders found that the soil was wet and hard to find stability upon. This caused those early architects to design new methods of building that would allow the buildings to extend well into the sky and not sink into the earth itself.

There was a time when the land ended much closer than it does now before going into the water of Lake Michigan. However, the city was growing faster than it had room. City planners eventually decided to start dumping tons of earth and sand and whatever else they could find into the lake. They eventually extended the city several blocks further into the lake, creating new land and new space to build parks and other buildings.

Chicago does have fault lines surrounding it. However, they are generally small, fairly stable, and don't do much in the way of damage when they do move. However, at times, the city has shaken a bit. New Madrid, Missouri, is a few hundred miles away and the site of the largest inland fault in the world. When earthquakes have hit there, they have shaken and rung church bells as far away as Boston. Still, Chicago has very little to worry about when it comes to the earth's wrath in that way.

The land around Chicago is also very flat. There are no mountains rising from the earth like the fingers of giant, long-buried gods. There are hills, of course, and times when rains cause those hills to move, but the chances of avalanches or mud-slides in Chicago are slim.

If there is a common threat from the earth in Chicago, it comes from the streets every spring. During the winter the cold causes the pavement to freeze. Water from the snow seeps into the cracks and crevices on the worn roads. When the snow plows come past, they tear up the asphalt. The changes in temperature then add to the problem. As the water filling the cracks melts, it leaves gaps that then become holes. As the saying goes in Chicago, there is winter and then there is pot-hole season. Still, none of these holes has ever grown to the point where it swallowed a man or a vehicle whole.

No, the biggest threat from the earth is when the most primal of earth's powers turns against the people. When gravity itself becomes a problem, the consequences can be deadly. Buildings, as strong as they may be, are built by humans from all-too-human materials, and they have accidents, show signs of weakness, or become faulty due to human negligence.

Chapter Eighteen

The Stadium

Chicago has its share of sports stadiums these days. However, there was a time when to see a sports team or concert, you really had to go downtown. As the suburbs began to expand ever westward, the need to bring entertainment for both sports fans and music fans closer to the residents grew. The large amounts of empty space near O'Hare Airport seemed like a perfect place to build a new stadium.

The area was in the northwest suburban area known as Rosemont. The most famous thing about the suburb, for a long time, was a huge water tower painted green all the way up to the top where it was painted red. Now, it seemed the perfect place for a new sports stadium. It would be known, initially, as the Rosemont Horizon.

The problem was that the location would put the stadium directly in the path of one of the busiest runways at O'Hare. The planes would almost appear to be landing directly on the roof of the place as the end of the runway was directly across the highway that whizzed past the new stadium. It would be difficult to build the stadium and make it so the jet engines would not interfere with the sports teams and performances happening inside.

It was decided that the huge beams that would arch over the stadium floor and the seats below would be made from wood. The wood would help dampen the sound, absorbing most of the noise. Other materials throughout the building would also be designed to absorb the sound and nearly completely tune out the jumbo jets flying only a few dozen feet above the roof.

Initially, the stadium was to be the location of a World Hockey League minor league team. However, before the stadium was completed, the entire league folded and the team never came into being. Still, there were other teams waiting to find a new home that would allow them to reach their intended audience.

Building a Disaster

So, construction began. The stadium would be large, but perhaps not as large as the Chicago Stadium downtown or any of the baseball stadiums. The stadium would hold about 20,000 people. Still, it was a large building, requiring massive concrete supports to give reinforcement and structure to the huge beams that would make up the roof, high above the stadium floor.

Construction began in the late seventies. It was ninety percent complete on August 14, 1979. The outside structure was completed and the huge beams were being installed across the floor. The beams were to be made of three huge pieces of lumber. There were to be sixteen glue-laminated wooden beams that would make up the roof. Each piece of lumber was 6.1 feet deep and would span the 288 feet across the stadium seats and the floor below. At the end of each support, there would be concrete columns to help keep them up.

By August 14th, one third of the beams had been installed. The wooden arches were tied up by girders which were interspersed by sets of three purlins. Iron, known as "angle irons," were to be used to hold the arches and girders in their proper place. Those angle irons were to be held in place by three bolts. However, a fateful decision was made during the placement of the arches and with the bolts.

The engineer supervising the construction decided that leaving out two of the bolts would be acceptable. The idea was to let the wood deform in a downward motion enough that would then make installing the remaining bolts easier. To compensate for the loss of the bolts, an outside contractor was hired to create steel plates to connect the arches and the girders.

There were no tall buildings around the construction site. On one side was a busy highway. There were industrial parks on all of the other sides. There was nothing to stop the wind from blowing straight through the girders, putting additional stress on arches that were already overtaxed and burdened without the proper supports.

It was Monday, August 14, 1979. The workers were on the beams, continuing to install the wood beams and inserting the bolts. However, the wind was blowing, and the planes were flying overhead. Suddenly, without warning, the wooden roof began to groan and then it fell. With a huge crash the wooden beams crashed straight down into the floor of the stadium. It took workers with it, killing five and injuring sixteen more.

As the rescue workers sorted through the rubble, the investigation began at the same time by the Occupational Safety and Health

Administration. They began to look at the beams, and the problem soon became obvious. The decision to leave out the bolts was the fatal flaw.

Over fifty-three percent of the bolts that connected the beams was missing. There were 944 bolts required for the beams to be safe. However, once the beams were studied, only 444 bolts could be found installed properly. Even of those that were installed, 338 had no nuts, and even of those nuts that were installed, many of them were only tightened using fingers instead of power tools. The entire network and webbing of wooden beams was completely unstable and could not possibly stand the added pressure of wind and sound produced in that area.

The steel plates that had been made to make up for the missing bolts were studied next. It soon became obvious that the workers had not been bothering to install the plates meant to hold up the beams in place of the bolts. Only twenty-seven percent of the steel plates that should have been in place actually were.

The main cause of the collapse was the poor installation of the bolts and the brackets. This created insufficient support for the beams. However, further investigations showed that there was inadequate bracing and the workers were storing tools and materials on the beams, adding weight to the structure.

Arena Moves On

OSHA ended up fining the company erecting the roof. They also fined the architect for the project and the subcontractors. Even the firm that was brought in to do the investigation was fined by OSHA for exposing their employees to unnecessary hazards during their inspections.

Of course, the roof was eventually completed on the stadium. One year after the roof collapsed, concrete stands that were under construction collapsed and dumped thirty-four tons of concrete into the basement. No one was hurt in that accident.

The stadium was completed. It has now become the All-State Arena—once corporate sponsorship for stadiums became the norm. The complex opened and sports teams did move in. For a time, the city's indoor soccer team called it home. Then the Chicago Wolves minor league hockey team moved in. Concerts and flea markets are also held inside and outside the stadium. The planes still fly overhead, sometimes appearing as if they are landing directly in the parking lot. However, the lessons had been learned on that fatal and fateful day. It cost the lives of five construction workers, but safety at the sight was improved and the stadium built. There have been no further accidents or collapses at the stadium.

Chapter Nineteen

The Party and the Porch

The area of Chicago known as Lincoln Park has long been the center for youthful activity. It is predominantly populated by students going to and from classes. While the rents may not be the cheapest in the city, they are generally more affordable than rents closer to downtown. They are also within easy reach of downtown, public transportation, and many of the more popular night-time venues the city has to offer.

Lincoln Park is also known for the relative beauty and wealth in its architecture and buildings. The houses along some streets are impressively large, but due to the limitations of being in the city when it comes to width, many of these homes are very long and several stories high.

Some of the apartment buildings are historical. They have been renovated and re-renovated many times to make room for more and more modern amenities. These include balconies and large wooden porches that crawl up the backs of most of the apartment buildings throughout the city, but in particular, the Lincoln Park area.

Most of the time the porches are big enough for the residents and maybe a few guests to use as a kind of balcony with a barbecue. Normally, there are wooden stairs leading up to the second floor landing. Here, there will be a large flat space where the back entrance to the apartment exists and enough space for parties and residents to use it for various purposes. Then there are more stairs and more landings, leading all the way to the top floor where there is usually the most space for any party-goers who might leak out from the apartment onto the porches.

In general, very few people stop to think about the porches they are standing on. They assume that the building is built solidly and that there are procedures and inspections in place to ensure their safety. Besides, most of the wood looks solid enough.

The Party

This was certainly the thought on June 29, 2003, at an apartment building on the north side. The second and third floors were being used for a party. Most of those in attendance knew each other from New Trier High School and Lake Forest High School which was also located on the city's north side. They were mostly in their early twenties and trying to reunite after heading off to colleges in the city and other parts of the country.

The apartments were full. The night was pleasant and not too hot, so it was natural that party-goers would eventually spill out onto the decks and porches that clung to the back of the building. As the crowd grew, so did the gathering on the balconies. Several witnesses said, afterward, that things did not feel safe and stable on the porches. However, some said that the construction and the wood looked new and stable. Others said they were concerned that the porches seemed to be moving and creaking.

There were about fifty people on the third floor balcony when things went wrong. According to witnesses who stood inside, facing the balcony, they heard a terrible cracking sound and the sound of splintering wood. Then, as they stood in mute horror, the people standing on the deck simply fell from sight. The porch collapsed.

The porch below, on the second floor, was also full of party-goers. The top porch fell directly on top of that porch. Then, the second floor porch collapsed onto the first floor porch. In each case, the horrible sound of splintering wood was heard again and again as the porches pulled down the entire wooden structure, causing the mass of humans and wood to fall into the basement. In total, about 100 people were smashed between the porches and mixed in with the splintered wood as it fell.

The night air was now filled with screams. Survivors began trying to pull people from the rubble. One of the survivors happened to be a nurse and she began to perform life-saving rescue efforts on those who were pulled from the wreckage. Rescue workers were called and the fire department arrived in minutes. The firemen pulled out chainsaws and began cutting through the tons of wood to try and get to the broken, bleeding, and pleading survivors trapped in the wreckage.

When the rubble was cleared away there were eleven dead that very night, their bodies broken beyond repair as they were pulled from the mess. Two more would die from their injuries in the coming days. Fifty-seven people were injured to varying degrees, but would live on with only their nightmares as souvenirs from that night.

Investigations Into Building Construction

Before too long, the city wanted to know why this had happened. At first, fire and rescue officials said it simply looked like a case of too many people crammed into a space that was never designed for that many people. However, as the investigation into the building, the landlords, and the recent renovations that had been done continued, more sinister problems began to appear.

In 1998, a permit had been issued to the LG Properties who owned the building. That permit was to install furnaces, some air conditioners and some new water heaters. Nowhere on that paper did it permit the owners to build balconies. However, permission was given by the building owners for the contractors to build new porches and balconies behind the building. Those new balconies would make the apartments that much more rentable and popular.

There are standards in the city for porches of that nature. The porches here violated many of those standards. For example, the balconies jutted out eleven feet from the building when the standards only permitted ten. The total area of the balcony was 231 square feet. This was 81 feet larger than permitted by the city. To top things off, the construction was shoddy. The supports used were inadequate for the size. The lengths of wood used to make up the floors of the balconies were smaller than regulation required. Finally, the balconies were attached to the building with screws that were far too short for the loads they were expected to bear. It was an accident waiting to happen, but that wasn't the end of it.

The porches had undergone inspections before. Each time they had been declared safe. Further investigations showed that the inspector in charge of certifying the porches at that location was new, woefully under-qualified, and not prepared to do his job.

The city sued the owners of the building and cited the breeches in the city ordinances that they felt resulted in the collapse. LG Properties was named in the suit along with Philip Pappas and George Koutroumos, the contractors who had built the porches and balconies in the first place. The city spent time and money inspecting other porches that had been built by Pappas and LG Properties. They discovered more violations.

As for Pappas, he claimed overcrowding was the problem, not his construction. An undercover investigation by a local media outlet showed that he had installed "no partying" signs on other properties he owned and meant it specifically for the balconies. Pappas also said that some witnesses claimed party-goers were jumping on the balcony just before it collapsed.

Lawsuits Arrive

In fact, the city did file a lawsuit, claiming negligence, against two survivors. William Fenton-Hathaway and John Koranda were charged because witnesses said they had been the ones doing the jumping on the porch just before it collapsed. John Koranda's brother, Robert, was killed in the accident.

No criminal charges were ever brought against anyone for the collapse. Pappas was ultimately fined $108,000 for the event. More lawsuits, these brought by families, were filed against Pappas and against the city for their poor inspection policies. The amounts won or negotiated in those cases are kept sealed.

The balcony was eventually rebuilt. The apartment was deemed uninhabitable for a time, but eventually the apartments were re-opened. The second balcony was made out of metal instead of wood. The city also instituted new policies for inspecting balconies and new rules for the amount of experience needed to be an inspector for balconies.

Conclusion

Fire, Water, Air and Earth

The city of Chicago has been through ups and downs just like most major cities. The strange thing about it, however, is how each of the disasters lead to greater things for the city and, at times, even helped the rest of the world. For some reason, the disasters and crises experienced by a city most people fly over and few think about outside of the Midwest, were so shocking, so powerful, and they electrified the country to such a degree, that steps were taken to make sure such disasters never happened again anywhere else.

After the massacre at Fort Dearborn, attention was drawn to an area of the country that most probably never thought about. They suddenly knew about the small trading post that had become a fort. As the country desired to expand, it was now a perfect place to expand into. Before too long the city of Chicago was one of the fastest growing in the country and, at one point, the western-most city for the entire country.

Of course, this then lead to the next big disaster. As the city grew, it began to grow faster than technology and safety could keep up. As such, the city had more wood and improper building materials than was safe. It was only a matter of time before a spark would cause a fire that would threaten the entire city. Thus, the rapid expansion of the city ultimately lead to the Great Chicago Fire.

Once the last embers of the fire had died down and the rebuilding started, the city came back stronger than ever. Before too long, the city was developing the first skyscrapers and advancing the technology involved in building bigger, better, stronger offices and buildings, and this lead to the creation of the supposedly fireproof theater. Of course, the fire there and the many dead women and children on that terrible matinee lead to changes across the country in how theaters were built and how they could be filled safely. Once again, it took the deaths of many to lead to changes to make things safe for everyone.

The fire that took the lives of so many in the school known as Our Lady of Angels shocked the world. Even the Pope took notice of the tragedy and responded. The world had continued to advance, but had left key safety issues in the past, such as with the schools. It took the deaths of many children to make people realize that things needed to change. Once again, things changed for the country and the rest of the world.

Within the city itself there were plans with the trolley system and those who felt that the city could only expand and continue by doing other things. It took the deaths of more innocent people to change the direction of the entire city. It was more fire that lead to changes for the city and safety for commuters.

Although the fresh water tidal waves had hit the Chicago area and areas along Lake Michigan had happened before, it was so rare that very few people thought about it. It took a freak afternoon and the deaths of fishermen to make weathermen and those who predicted those events take notice and start to issue warnings. Now the shorelines along the Lake were safer for those bathing or fishing.

Another disaster in another body of water and in another part of the world contributed, in some way, toward the deaths of hundreds of people, wiping out entire families, with the sinking of a ship chartered for a company picnic. The way in which Christmas was celebrated changed with the deaths of innocent men just trying to deliver trees. When the flood shut down the entire city the city stepped in to help and prevent such a thing from happening ever again.

At one time, the entire world was moving toward airships as the prominent mode of transportation. In fact, the plan was for Chicago to become the Midwest center for airship travel. It took a spectacular crash and the deaths of workers in a bank to change the course of the city. This lead to the development of airfields like Midway and O'Hare and turning them into world-class airports.

Once O'Hare became the busiest airport in the world—it was really only a matter of time before an accident happened. On that day in early spring when Flight-191 went down, it shook the entire country. Over 200 people died so that the DC-10 could be looked at again, changes made, and safety increased for passengers flying to all parts and points in the country.

Very little can be done to prevent weather. Chicago sits in an area prone to severe weather in both summer and winter. The best that can be hoped for is that the people who predict the weather will be able to foresee the danger and provide adequate warning. It took the deaths of far too many, and far too many of them children, to realize that there were problems with the system in place.

After the rubble was cleared, the bodies removed, and the winds had died down, the processes taken to ensure that such disasters would not happen again helped other large cities in the area. In fact, it lead to policies by the National Weather Service that make life in all cities a bit safer. On the backs of those who died, the world country was made a bit safer.

At times, despite being well away from mountains and fault lines, the earth reaches up and tries to grab structures to pull them down. Most of the time, however, the earth is helped by negligence on the part of human beings. In those cases, people were brought to justice or fined. Improvements were made to make the structures safer for apartment dwellers and construction workers. Yes, it took lives to make those improvements, but Chicago seems to want to take its blood before making things better.

Chicago is a world class city. It has a world class art museum and orchestra. It has some of the greatest architecture that the world has ever seen. It has world-class sports teams. It stands beside the greatest cities of the world. It took time, and it took effort and, sadly, it took some mistakes that cost people their lives.

But out of the ashes and tears, Chicago rises like the phoenix, taking seriously its past disasters, and welcoming in a new and improved day.

Bibliography

"A Theater Horror." *Moberly Daily Monitor* December 31, 1903.

Allsopp, Jim. "40th Anniversary of Northern Illinois' Worst Tornado Disaster." http://www.crh.noaa.gov/108/severe/21Apr1967_tornado.pdf.

Bales, Richard F. "Did the Cow Do It? A New Look at the Cause of the Great Chicago Fire" http://www.thechicagofire.com.

Bobula, Thomas. "Seiches." Encyclopedia of Chicago.

Chicago Historical Society. "The Great Conflagration." http://www.chicagohs.org/fire/conflag/essay-2.html.

Chicago Public Radio. "Remembering the Loop Flood." http://www.chicagopublicradio.org/Print.aspx?audioID=10023.

Chicago Daily Tribune, July 26, 1919. "11 Witnesses Say Fire Began in Blimp's Nose."

CNN.com. "Chicago high-rise fire injures 37." http://cnn.usnews.printthis.clickability.com/pt/cpt?action=cpt&title=CNN.com+-+Chicago.

Cowan, David and Jon Kuenster. " To Sleep with the Angels: The Story of a Fire." Ivan. R. Dee, publisher, August 25, 1998.

"Dying Alone: An Interview with Eric Kleinenberg author of Heat Wave: A Social Autop Disaster in Chicago." http://www.press.uchicago.edu/Misc/Chicago/443213in.html.

Earle, Howard, "Disaster attends a matinee" *Family Weekly*, December 28, 1958.

Graczyk, Jim. "The Christmas Tree Captain." http://www.ghostguides.com/christmas html.

Great Lakes Monitoring. "The Fate of the Christmas Tree Ship." http//www.epa.gov/g monitoring/great_minds_great_lakes/history/christmas_tree.html.

Groves, Adam. "Cook County Administration Building Fire," http://www.ideals.uiuc bitstream/handle/2142/97/Cook%20County%20Administration%20Building%20Fire 2003.pdf?sequence=2.

"Hotel LaSalle." http://chicago.urban-history.org/sites/hotels/lasalle.htm.

Illinois State Geological Survey. "Seiches: Sudden, Large Waves a Lake Michigan Dan http://www.isgs.uiuc.edu/sections/engin-coast/lakemich-coastal-seiches.shtml.

Johnson, Allan. "The Chicago Blizzard of 1967: Winter in Chicago has never been easy, bu' one was a record-setter." http://www.chicagotribune/com/news/politics/chi-chicago 1967blizzard-story,0,1032940.story.

Kilroy, Chris. "Special Report: American Airlines Flight 191." AirDisaster.com http://v airdisaster.com/special/special-aa191.shtml.

Kriz, Marjorie. "The Crash of the Wingfoot Air Express." Chicago Tribune, June 10, 197

Longacre, Glenn V. "The Christmas Tree Ship: Captain Herman E. Schuenemann an(Schooner Rouse Simmons." The U.S. National Archives & Records Administration.

Meincke, Paul. "40th anniversary of Chicago blizzard: Snow paralyzed city in 1967." h abclocal.go.com/wls/story?section=weather&id=4973699&pt=print.

Nazario, Carlos, "Rosemont Horizon Arena Timber Roof Collapse; Chicago." http://matd failurecases/Building%20Cases/rosemont_horizon_arena.htm.

O'Keefe, Phil. "The Green Hornet Streetcar Disaster." http://users.ameritech.net/sigri(grnhrnt.htm.

OLAfire.com. "One of the Worst School Fires In U.S. History." http://www.olafire.com/ Summary.asp.

Plainfield Public Library. "Tornado History." http://plainfield.lib.il.us/general/tornadohis asp.

Sares, Theodore. "The Day a 'Tidal Wave' Hit Chicago." Ezine Articles.com.

Taylor, Roy. "The 1990 Plainfield, IL Tornado." Roytalor.info http://www.roytaylor.inf(writing/plainfieldtornado1990.html.

Townson, Patrick. "The Great Chicago Flood of 1992." http://www.totse.com/en/politics/p cal_spew/chiflood.html.

Weird & Haunted Chicago. www.prairieghosts.com

Weird and Haunted Chicago. "The Trolley of Death: The Green Hornet Trolley Disaster." h www.prairieghosts.com/green_hornet.html.

Wikipedia.org. "1990 Plainfield tornado." http://en.wikipedia.org/wiki/Plainfield_Torna

Wikipedia.org. "1995 Chicago Heat Wave." http://en.wikipedia.org/wiki/Chicago_Heat_W of_1995.

Wikipedia.org. "2003 Chicago Balcony Collapse." http://en.wikipedia.org/wiki/2003_ cago_balcony_collapse.

Wikipedia.org. "American Airlines Flight 191." http://en.wikipedia.org/wiki/American lines_Flight_191.

Wikipedia.org. "Belvidere – Oak Lawn tornado outbreak." http://en.wikipedia.org/wiki/E dere_Tornado_Outbreak.

Wikipedia.org. "Chicago Flood." http://en.wikipedia.org/wiki/Chicago_Flood.

Wikipedia.org. www.wikipedia.org/wiki/Great_Chicago_Fire. "1871 Great Chicago Fire.'

Wikipedia.org. "Iroquois Theater Fire." http://en.wikipedia.org/wiki/Iroquois_Theater_F

Wikipedia.org. "Our Lady of Angels School Fire." http://en.wikipedia.org/wiki/Our_Lad: the_Angels_School_Fire.

Wikipedia.org. "United Airlines Flight 553." http://en.wikipedia.org/wiki/United_Airl: Flight_553.